Gatherings

A Collection of Writing Genre

Gatherings

A Collection of Writing Genre

Anthony J. Marsella

MOUNTAIN ARBOR
PRESS

*Waste no more time arguing about what
a good man should be. Be one!*

**Marcus Aurelius
(121 CE – 180 CE)**

MOUNTAIN ARBOR
PRESS

ISBN: 978-1-63183-023-5
Library of Congress Control Number: 2016905886

10 9 8 7 6 5 4 3 2   0 5 0 3 1 6

Printed in the United States of America

♾This paper meets the requirements of ANSI/NISO Z39.48-1992 (Permanence of Paper)

To Family, Friends, Colleagues, Strangers . . .

That you may know me through words

Table of Contents

Preface
The Context of Contents

Words, Writing, Genre . . .

This volume is a gathering of my writing in differing expressive genre. It is for me, a celebration of words; words embracing moments and years, reality as I experienced it, tolls and hopes, clashes of opportunity and character; restorative moments of unrestrained imagination, all freeing mind for sharing.

Some entries in this collection were published previously in two of my volumes under Aurelius Press (*Poems across Time and Place: A Journey of Heart and Mind; War, Peace, Justice: An Unfinished Tapestry*), and also in Transcend Media Services (**www.transcend.org**). The prior entries are old friends, remaining with me, anchors of place and time.

My decision to publish this collection grew from my delight in discovering the virtues of writing in different genre. The majority of entries are poetry; however, there are also poetic lyrics, poetic elegies, short stories, and political essays. Within the broader poetry genre, I discovered opportunities for different voices, ranging from delicate and sensitive, to assertive and challenging. The discoveries were exhilarating: I could express myself in varying formats and styles.

There were times I began writing a poem, expecting only to write a few verses, and then finding my words growing in proportion and consequence, unstoppable streams of insights, nuances, and details. The brief poem became an elegy or a short story.

An example of this is my elegiac poem, *Artist in Agony*. What began as a description of my Sicilian step-father's experiences as an immigrant pursuing a better life in the United States of America, soon became testimony to the enduring scars inscribed in his life in mid-20th Century Europe. The wars and ideological conflicts required words describing this tragic and inescapable crucible for his life. A elegiac poem emerged; insufficient, but now a beginning of a yet longer story to be told.

I came, in time, to understand my step-father's deep sense of grief and loss. He found neither the peace nor opportunity he sought in his immigration to the United States. He could not escape the legacy of his tormented past. He died in my arms, whispering: "Life's tragedy is that so many people are never given an opportunity to develop their talent." My words honor him.

Gatherings . . .

In those special moments when words begin to order emotions and crystallize thoughts, I was pushed and pulled to capture the rush of "unfolding" experiences, an inspiring synergy -- a coming together -- a synoptic view of my life. For me, **"Gatherings,"** is the right title for this collection! It is about connections! It is about the power of gathering words to explore, unrestrained by a single form of expression.

I want readers to enter my life -- to know me through my writing. Pablo Neruda, the Chilean Nobel Laureate, wrote a poem entitled, **"The Word,"** published in his volume, *Full Powers* (1962). It is a salute to "words." In his closing lines, Neruda heralds the birth of *the first word*. He writes:

Still the atmosphere trembles
*   With the first word*
*   Produced with panic and groaning,*
*   It emerged from the darkness*
*   And even now there is no thunder*
*   That thunders with the iron sound*
*   Of that word,*

The first word uttered:
Perhaps it was just a whisper, a raindrop,
But its cascade still falls and falls.

Gracias, Neruda! You unleashed a crescendo of understanding, insight, and wisdom, all to be found in words. Words are the "alphabet" of life! Gather your words; explore insight, emotion, and meaning! **Alchemy**!

Nature

Bumble Bee: An Elegy

I.

You ask what I do as I sit alone in my house,
    Gazing at life through cathedral windows,
        Clean, clear, translucent,
            Gift of rain!

I watch bumble bees hover,
    Rise and fall,
        Define their place and space;
            Primitive reflexes -- procreation and defense;
            Generations pursued,
                A natural order!

Bumble bees circle,
    Soar, loop, dive,
        With precision;
            No path the same,
                Eluding prediction!

For a millisecond . . . contact!
    Separation,
        Distance,
            Connection,
                Again, again, again,
                Dominance!
                Submission!
                    "No! . . . No!
                    Life!"

Destiny's timeless presence!
   Forged across generations,
      Harmony with place:
         "I watch in awe . . ."

Bumble bees charge my windows,
   Attacking duplicate-foe images,
      No recognition of self,
         Not unlike humans;
            Reflexive responses to known color, shape, size!
            Fixed behavior!
               Limiting choice!

Thump! Thump! Thump!
   Encounters with reflections of unyielding rivals!
      "I will defend my seed!
         Be gone interloper!
            I protect vessel and progeny!
               "I am creation!"

"This is my space!
   I was sired here!
      Last year,
         The year before that!
            And before that year!
               Wooden holes -- my womb!
               Know your peril!"

Flights!
   Attacks!
      Ballets in space!
         Pirouettes,
            Choreographed by . . . Balanchine?
               Did he observe bees?

How easy to assign conscious intent!
   Willful choices across species,
      A human impulse!
         Anthropomorphism!
            "Aha! I see what you are doing!
            Love in the afternoon!
            How clever you are!
            I see the dance."

Each day . . .
   A repeat!
      Pollen mists now added to the dance.
         Oak, pine, maple spores dust the air.
            Veils of food - succor - nectar!
               Wings weighted!
                  "Behold my strength!
                  I still fly!"

Spring's ancient ritual visible!
   The bumble bee:
      Attacking! Defending,
         Mating! Partnering!
            Accepting! Rejecting!
               "How do bees choose mates?
                  Do bumble bees know ecstasy?
                  I do!"

II.

Days pass, night arrives;
   A fallen bumble bee on my deck!
      Covered in golden pollen,
         A seasonal shroud!
            Yesterday, worn with pride!
               Today, death's blanket!

I gaze – hesitant – entranced:
    Delicate beauty!
        Black and yellow furred body,
            Diaphanous wings,
                Bulging black eyes!
                    I witness, I behold . . .
                        "An honorable end!"

The source of yesterday's drama!
    Now apparent!
        Author, producer, director . . . at rest!
        Motionless body!

Should I grasp nature's delicate gift?
    Carry corporeal remains to rail's edge?
    Release to earth's collected debris?

Is something more demanded?
    Something praising nature's intent!
        Something honoring fertility flights!
        Sacred sensuality!
            Perpetuating life!
                Renewing purpose!

What brought this sad end?
    Reflecting cathedral windows?
        Endless collisions with self,
            No awareness of folly?
                Like man,
                    Failing to know within . . . without!

Am I to blame?
    Did my presence interfere?
        Windows alien to fixed instincts!
            Anthropocene assault!
                Another victim now apparent!
                Perpetrator . . . ?

Yesterday, wasps entered bumble-bee space!
  Stream-lined presence,
    Sleek black-bodies,
      Brown wings:
        Quick!
          Stinger visible!
          Enemy!

Lesson here:
  Who . . . what . . . claimed victory?
  Who . . . what claimed death?
  Life struggles fought!
    Is fatigue to blame?
      Fulfilled purpose?
        Primal order!
        Mystery!

I do not disturb the lifeless bumble bee
  In its pollen shroud!
    Time needed for thought.
      How to demonstrate respect?
      How do I honor life?
      Mate and progeny
        Now burrowed in wooden-deck holes!
        Awaiting instinct to emerge!

No more thumps!
  Echoes only!
    A ceremonial drum!
      No trumpet "Taps"
      For bumble bees!

Should others gather?
  Create buzzing harmony?
    Whirl, dance, dive,
      Salute,

Depart -- raised wings?
Disposal left to chance?

III.

Rains came today!
Heavy torrents,
Rinsing pollen-covered surfaces,
Baptizing a lifeless bumble bee;
Jordan's waters –
Rinsing,
Blessing aspirant!

I leave remains untouched!
Scene serene:
Rain-washed body
Purging wounds!
Rinsing life scars!
Purpose fulfilled!
And next Spring?
Amen!

Comment:

I began collecting words for what I saw occurring on my deck on April 10, 2015. I watched for weeks as a cycle of bumble bee life unfolded outside my windows -- an entire cycle creating a new generation who would re-enact the drama next year. There was something sacred about the life-play I beheld: actors, parts, behaviors, drama, end . . . applause, prayer! Shakespeare would have loved it, turning into a human drama of love and death, of kings and villains, of life as an endless creation saga.

Autumn Brook

I.

The autumn brook is alive,
　　Bubbling, rippling, streaming,
　　　　Knowing its fate!
　　　　　　Accepting, weighing, enduring,
　　　　　　　　Amid signs of inevitable change,
　　　　　　　　　　Inscribed by nature,
　　　　　　　　　　　　Beyond recourse!

Conscious instinct:
　　Position of sun in sky,
　　　　Night temperatures,
　　　　　　Falling leaves,
　　　　　　　　Saturated debris!

Fish seeking refuge,
　　Amid rocks and stones!
　　　　Safety in shadows!
　　　　　　Darting for food,
　　　　　　　　Quick return,
　　　　　　　　　　Silver flashes,
　　　　　　　　　　　　Visible to frog glances.

II.

Centuries of memory inscribed in autumn brook's flow,
　　Awareness ... gleaned from a thousand sources,
　　　　In water ... on banks,
　　　　　　A known inscribed sun-dial,

Time-tested algorithms,
Mysteries only to man!

Flow continues!
Blocked by beaver dams!
New paths form,
Implicit purposes engraved in watery course.

The autumn brook signals:
The time has come.
It is upon us,
Recognized,
Undeniable,
Inevitable!

At the cusp of change,
Fusion of disparate harbingers,
Submission!
Delicacy in presence,
Whispering current,
Partnership in purpose,
With distant shores!

Comment:

There are oceans, rivers, streams, and brooks. All share Earth's passing seasons, all serve mighty and lesser purposes; all inscribe and shape life in different ways. I find the brook to be fascinating. The brook exists across different seasons; but it is perhaps in August, as the season unfolds in preparation for winter, the brook's presence alert, becomes one with all about it.

SHE IS A FLOWER

She is a flower!
    I do not understand the mystery,
        Her transformation of body and spirit!
           Reality transcended!
             Metaphysical truth!

She became a flower before me!
    I watched in amazement,
        Witnessing unfolding petals, pistils,
           Radiant blossoming of promise!
             Inviting . . . union!

As a child,
    She would stand before flowers,
        Gazing!
           Beholding!
           Becoming!

She dismissed calls to leave her gifted presence:
    "Come!
        Enough!
           Dinner now!"

"No!"
    She replied defiantly!
        "Time is to be filled with beauty!
           It is not to be wasted!"

"I cannot leave;
    The flower is not yet fixed in my mind,
        An imprint must be inscribed!
           Remaining forever,
              Archetype!
                I will know!"

Amid a flower's peak color and fragrance,
    She would speak:
        "I know you!"
           I remember you!"
              You are as beautiful as the flower
                You replaced."

She would smell the flower,
    Pressing its center to her face,
        Not as a stranger,
           Intruding . . . defiling,
              But as a gifted joining,
                Fulfilling nature's intent!

She would become the flower!
    Entering its presence!
        Transcending boundaries!
        Union!

Inhaling its heady scent,
    Time . . . place vanished.
        Delicate, pungent,
           Simple, complex,
              Pure, cleansing!
                Ancient ties renewed!

II.

In school she would draw flowers,
    Nothing more!

Teachers urged other topics upon her!
   She would smile,
      "I love flowers!"

Recognizing her fascination,
   Her captivation,
      Kind voices would say:
         "I know you love flowers!
            They are important for you!
               There is something about them,
                  For you, in you!
                     Can you tell me?"

She would smile at the voice,
   Acknowledging question,
      Resisting reply!
         Can enchantment be answered in words?
            Does my face not show magic?

She had become a flower!
   Do they not understand?
      Incarnation!
         Life as life!
            She was drawing existence;
               Drawing . . . herself,
                  And more!

Later, in art school, now a talented artist,
   Flowers remained her passion.
      Forms, colors, fragrances,
         Etched in mind and hand!

When nude models came to art class,
   She painted them, as she saw them:
      Men, women, black, white,
         As flowers!

Unfolding stems for limbs
Leaves adorning hair,
Mists rising from petal skin!

III.

There are flower gardens in her yard,
Flower paintings in her home,
Flower-filled vases,
And a single flower in her hair
Worn above her ear!

"Why do you love flowers so much, Mommy?"
Her daughter asks.
She smiles at the question:
Innocent! Pure!

"Yes, my beautiful flower:
I love flowers;
They are delicate and fragile,
Strong and weak,
Giving love, needing love,
Like you!
Like me;
That is why I love them!"

"I like your big painting of the white rose, Mommy!
With the hummingbird flying above it;
Waiting, as if it knows it should enter,
But wanting to choose . . .
Just the right time . . . and place!"

"That is my favorite painting, too!"

"What does the hummingbird do?

"The hummingbird enters the heart of the flower.
    Hovering:
        It senses it is the right place to be,
            The flower welcomes entry."

Comment:

This poem became for me so much more than words about the beauty of flowers. Within the span of day, the poem grew into testimony about life, love, and connection. Unbounded existence! Becoming one!

I SEE OTTER IN YOU

I.

I see **Otter** in you:
    In the watery blue of your eyes,
        In your intense gaze,
            Gentle grin,
                Constant smile!

I see **Otter** in you:
    In your readiness to frolic,
        In your knowledge of delight,
            In your effortless entry into fantasy,
                And prompt return,
                    With a stare!

I see **Otter** in you:
    As you search corners of your mind,
        Patient, alert, aware, mindful,
            Warrior when needed,
                Anticipating the possible,
                    Sensing hints for survival.

II.

Otter:
    You are the stuff of legends!
        Mythic in tales,
            Storied archetype!
                Present in clouds, rivers, minds.

Otter:

> You are prized across the world:
>> Celtic, Norse, Aboriginal, American Indian.
>>> Home in water, earth, and skies.

Otter:

> You are privileged by gods and spirits,
>> Topic of creation myths, poems, fables.
>>> Remembered in storied hymns and songs!

II.

I see **Otter** in you:

> As you cup your hands,
>> Bring them to your face,
>>> Tasting, inhaling, drinking . . . savoring!

Then:

> A nimble lick of your finger tips,
>> A return to cupped hands,
>>> Deep thought,
>>>> Prayer!

I see **Otter** in you:

> Mischief in your smile,
>> Reflex in your movement,
>>> Purpose in your glance,
>>>> Never caprice,
>>>>> Never malevolence!

I see **Otter** in you,

> Inherent trust,
>> Abiding confidence,
>>> Transcending time and place!

You have known love,

> Given love,
>> No hesitancy, doubt, or question.

I see **Otter** in you,
　　Desire to bring delight,
　　　　Love for those in your open house,
　　　　　　Whether lair, den, or matted leaves.

I see **Otter** in you,
　　In willingness to play,
　　　　To help, to care
　　　　　　To share!

III.

I see **Otter** in you:
　　As you walk, not swim,
　　　　Speak, not bark.
　　　　　　Touch, not lick.
　　　　　　　　And caress your mate,

I see **Otter** in you:
　　Instincts for attachment,
　　　　Reflexes,
　　　　　　Un-thought,
　　　　　　　　Natural,
　　　　　　　　　　Desire!

Your totem could be other things,
　　Animals, birds, mythic figures, contrived creations,
　　　　No! No! It is **Otter!**
　　　　　　Do **Otters** bite?

Comments:

Sometimes the only way to describe a person's nature is by finding it in something natural -- an animal, tree, or stream. It is nature's way of asserting identity in all things - - of revealing connections.

Exploring Ideas

- *Cognito Ergo Sum!*
- Relinquishing Human Identity
- Asian Thought: *Unraveling Knots*
- *Lifeism*: Beyond Humanity

Cognito Ergo Sum!

I think, therefore I am!
   I am, therefore I think!
      I think I am!

I think of others!
   I think others think!
      I am thinking others thinking!
         I am what others think!
            I want to think what others think!
            I want others' thinking!

I think thinking is not thought!
   I think thinking is life!
      I think life is reflexive!
         It feeds upon itself!
            Seeking, exploring, becoming!

Thought is not thinking!
   Thought is thinking's content!
      Inborn and acquired,
         In constant flux,
            Memory, image, sensation!
               Captive to muscle, viscera, emotion!
               Atomistic, quantum, mind!
               Escape thought?

What is the greatest thought?
   $E = MC^2 \cdots$ No!
      Quantum!
         Sermon on the Mount,
           Non-Violence!

Consciousness!
Morality – Justice!
DNA!
AI?
Big Bang!

Thinking is process!
Process is product!
Heisenberg!
I am what is!
I am bounded!
I am boundless!

I am what am!
"So sayeth the Lord!"
Who bounded --unbounded me?
Gifting me with thinking!
Casting me into infinity of thoughts!
Doubting knowing,
Knowing!
Life!

Who then knows thinking?
Eyes see!
Hearts know!
Essential thinking invisible!

I think, therefore I am!
I am, therefore I think!
I am what am!
So be it!

Comment:

What can be said? I say thank you to a gifted friend and student for patient conversations inspiring wisdom and thought. I thank her also for reminding me of Antoine de Saint-Exupery's, *The Little Prince*: "The essential is invisible to the eyes."

Relinquishing Human Identity

Unfolding Evolution Via
Bio-Metric Communication Technologies

Introduction

While no one can deny, the many contributions of bio-metric advances for human life: medicine, work, quality of life; we need to consider the consequences of technology out-pacing our abilities to grasp long-term impacts. This is especially true as developments in artificial intelligence move toward singularity, the term used for the point in time when robotic forms have parity with human brain functions and speeds.

In this context, I began to see ancient human impulses to create imaginary beings or mythological beings with unique powers, and skills (part animal-part human; part robot-part human), as a continuing reality for emerging developments in bio-technology.

Of special note is the technological survival of the fittest may be confined to those possessing the wealth, power, and position to exploit and to utilize resources for personal privilege and control (e.g., bio-technologies involving mass population cloning, use of bio-mechanical parts, storage of embryos and gametes, and inter-planetary colonization).

Terms of Reference

The following terms of reference represent a partial presentation of the various types and forms of mythologies and emerging technological realities. Whether in mythology or in science fiction publications and movies, these types and forms are important for us to recognize and acknowledge. They are creations of human thought.

Angels (Supernatural Beings, often humanoid in appearance, but with wings)

Bionic Man/Woman (Human with mechanical parts)

Bots (Any programmed forms)

Cartoon Heroes (e.g., Superman, Spider Man, Wonder Woman, Mighty Mouse)

Centaur (Mythical combination of a human and horse)

Chimera (Entities created by transplanting cells from different organisms in embryo stage)

Cloning (Reproduction of an organism from DNA)

Code (Programming of an object or task through use of 0 and 1 ordering)

Cyborg (Combining human and mechanical parts; in movies and cartoons, often hero/heroine)

Demons (Supernatural-evil beings! Often referred to in religion, and occult services)

Storage: Storage of life forms (e.g., bodies, gametes, embryos) via freezing, and other forms of perpetuating existence or possibilities of existence)

Greek & Roman Gods & Goddesses (Mythology)

Humanoids (Any entity resembling the physical appearance of a human being)

Hybrids (Combination of two or more forms or functions – hybrid autos, humans)

Isis (Bird/Human. Ancient Egyptian Goddess)

Mechanical Body Parts (e.g., Heart, kidney, limbs)

Minotaur (Mythical combination of human & bull)

NanoBots (Mechanical machines and robots driven by nanometers 10^{-9}; Also see nanoids, nanites. Size is reduced to "nano" level)

Robot (Programmed mechanical entities. Can assume human-like appearance or function)

Shiva (Multiple arms; Hindu deity)

Stem Cells (Cells capable of reproducing; building injured parts)

Synths (Terms used to refer to quasi-human robots capable of performing all human tasks, but programmed to lack emotion and to obey commands)

Super Athletes (Record holders and breakers in athletics and other contests)

Super-Humans (Humans with specialized talents exceeding "normal" limits)

Supreme Beings (God images and creations. Numerous supreme beings across human history)

Thor (Powerful Super God. Nordic deity)

Three-Dimensional Printer Reproduction (Printers can reproduce any part using appropriate organic or non-organic cellular material)

Transplants (Surgical replacement of organs taken from others [donators])

Zombies (A re-animated dead person. Zombies have become popular topics of TV series and movies)

Emerging Mechanisms for Technological Change

The evolutionary changes occurring, as partially listed above, constitute a spectrum of controls and futures for human behavior. Among these are terms absent from daily use by most citizens, but available to professionals working within this area.

- **Artificial intelligence (AI)**

- **Analytics** (information processing methods and procedures capable of informing the state or status of an object, including humans, even as great distances)

- **Algorithms** (Ordered chain of decision processes to resolve a problem)

- **Mathematical Procedures** (Predictive models, sorting and classifying algorithms)

- **Nanotechnology** (Existing capacity within ICT industries to reduce the size of information-communication technologies to miniscule sizes; this permits building of complex systems. A nano is 10^{-9} in size. Nano-technologies enable development of complex systems simultaneously capable of processing and holding vast amounts of content)

- **Sensors** (Materials capable of informing the status or state of an object, and thus enabling feedback to a control system)

- **Storage:** Enormous storage capacities for information and data (units of terabytes, not mega or gigabytes)

Why Diversity?

The world is now concerned about biological and cultural diversity. There are growing pressures for homogenization, and for destruction of existing natural and human resources. "Diversity," for me, is not simply a term to be discussed regarding the distribution of social, economic, and political power across various identity markers: gender, race, ethnicity, age, class, and so forth. For me, "diversity" is an inherent characteristic of all life. It is the defining characteristic of life.

In a paper on *"Lifeism,"* I state "Life" is not only life as we define in its biological descriptors such as "repair, "reproduction," digestion, and related processes; rather, "Life" is in the very process of cosmic creation, euphemistically called the "Big Bang Theory."

Of special interest, are the processes of fission (i.e., separation) and fusion (i.e., connection). Amidst the din of argument and debate on this topic, my view is the very moment of the creation of the universe(s) was "Life." There was and is, an unfolding life force, represented as fission and fusion; these are essential forces in our unfolding world, involving the evolution of humans and other life forms.

There are, of course, many more complexities regarding matter, energy, gravity, time, and god particles. At this point in time, and for my purposes, I think there is a presence of a "life force," inherent in the "big bang" itself, creating "diversity" in endless forms and processes -- organic and non-organic.

In brief, I am suggesting "diversity," in all of its representations, is a refection of life. Diversity is not to be dismissed in a quest for release from the discomfort of variations in favor of "uniformity" – order over chaos. Diversity exists from the smallest possible form and process, to diversity in biological, environmental, cultural, and national levels.

And here is the rub! Diversity -- biological, environmental, cultural, and national -- should be preserved, because destroying diversity in favor of uniformity or homogenization destroys variation. In variation are the seeds of choice and potential. Homogenization is pursued because it offers control over differences; "diversity," for all of its life preserving virtues, brings with it possibilities of "disorder," and even chaos." Decisions to impose order can exact unexpected damages and destruction.

For example, all societies require "order" to control differences. This order is pursued in social organization, and is institutionalized in schools, workplaces, and families. Eventually, if a society becomes a nation, the issue of differences becomes a major problem regarding national identity, and loyalty to societal principles. But, the more that we impose "order," (homogenization?), the more we limit options and choices. Octavio Paz, the Mexican Nobel Laureate, said: *"Life is diversity, death is uniformity."*

I raise serious questions about life and diversity regarding uniformity, and ultimately, the issue of human identity. I ask whether the phrase: "Human is, as human does," will be reduced to altered views of human nature. Clearly, increasing developments in mechanistic, technological, and robotic areas are bringing humans to the point of "singularity."

The term "singularity" is used by many to refer to the point in our near future when robots (i.e., mechanical units) are "equal" to humans in intelligence, and other processes and functions. Many authors are now writing of the consequences of technical developments. It is clear innovations emerge rapidly, while awareness of consequences is often far behind.

It is within this context of thought and concern I fear "homogenization!" In the fullest sense of the term, homogenization is erasing differences in favor of a emergent forms or substances easier to control, more efficient in management, production, capital exploitation, and value. Yes, we can homogenize cultures, biological life forms, and environments. In the process, uniformity is easier to control. But here we must ask, "Who is in control?" And we must ask, "why," and "what," does this control imply?

We are in a global era of interdependence, but the interdependence is under American hegemonic control, and the consequences are threatening "diversity." Existing wealth, power, and position sectors are controlling (destroying?) the world by encouraging increases in monopolization of critical sectors of our lives (e.g., Big Ag, Big Banks, Big Education, Big Government, Big Medicine, Big Pharm, Big Transportation, Big Beer).

I am raising the issue of whether the process of evolution – human evolution – is being directed by the past, yet pulled by an unfolding future, toward completely new human life forms of varying shapes, abilities, and behaviors; this is occurring even as we fail to understand the consequences.

The Artist: Prophet of Bio-Information Technology Control

In Stanley Kubrick's popular prophetic movie, *2001: A Space Odyessy*, the computer, HAL, a "heuristically" programmed algorithmic computer) (also obviously named for IBM by taking each subsequent letter in the alphabet), emerges as "sentient" form of artificial intelligence, controlling an exploratory space craft mission to Jupiter. At some point, however, HAL assumes "consciousness" as an "evil" force, propelled toward destruction for its (unknown) reasons.

There are many interpretations of the meaning of Arthur Clarke's volume as the basis of the movie 2001 and Kubrick movie. What is agreed, however, is both were exploring the emerging powers and consequences of artificial intelligence, and expressions and powers of robotics, bionics, hybrids, and automatons. Today, images and implications of these early fictional artistic creations are considered *passé*, as bio-technological changes in information processing and products have assumed new proportion and implication for our lives.

We are on the cusp of modifying human nature in unimaginable ways, far beyond cloning, far beyond genetic engineering and mod-ification, far beyond creating consciousness.

Science fiction, not to be undone, has given us scores of variations on human forms and capacity, often in the shape of man-made monsters and villains (e.g., Frankenstein, Vampires, Zombies), and more recently, robots and automatons with appealing and nefarious forms and capabilities (e.g., IBM's Watson, R2D2, the bionic man). Mary Shelley's classic 19th century book, *Frankenstein,* loomed as a prophetic recognition of the unlimited possibilities of humans crossing known thresholds in the creation of alternative human forms and processes.

Mary Shelley, like many others, saw the unfolding of industries and technologies, along with a human impulse to push the limits of imagination and creation. What could be imagined (e.g., flying), could be pursued with unknown and untold consequences! A new day was upon us! The current craze for zombies and for vampires is a remarkable example. I have not been able to understand their popularity except as an escape from a technical life, into alternative ways of being capable of surviving time and circumstance.

Mythology, Cartoons, and Hybrids

In a previous paper, *"Human is as Human Does: Reflections on Human Nature,"* I wrote mythology, cartoon figures, and science fiction have offered us an unlimited panorama of thought regarding human nature and possibilities. I noted we have gone from minotaurs and centaurs, to Superman and Spider Man, to a spectrum of biological and robotic advances including transplants, artificial organs, animal part transplants, hybrids, robotics, 3-D creations, clones, chimera, and now, complete surveillance and capturing of our identities.

Consider for example, mythological creatures merging human and animal forms, including the *minotaur* (i.e., half man and half bull), *centaur* (i.e., half human and half horse), *Goddess Isis* (i.e., bird-head and human body), *Goddess Shiva* (i.e., multiple arms), and gods and goddesses of all sizes, purposes, with capacities exceeding human limitations in body and mind (e.g., Zeus, Athena, Neptune).

Cartoon Figures

We are exposed daily to cartoon figures assuming human or quasi-human qualities. What is the consequence of this constant daily exposure? Even as I write of robots (i.e., mechanical beings), there is the issue of making humans mechanical, through highly developed behavior control methods actively employed by national govern-ments and private contractors for their purposes.

Cartoon figures build upon imagination. They give us super-heroes and super–villains who possess virtually every conceivable special ability (e.g., strength, flying, wisdom, moral or immoral code), played out in a constant struggle between good and evil. These cartoon figures (e.g., Superman, Wonder Woman, Green Hornet, Road Runner) come to the fore, calling attention to our human needs, insecurities, and limitations.

We mere mortals are envious of their abilities, skills and roles. Think how often, as children, we played these figures, dressing in capes, Halloween costumes, and masks and painted faces. And let us not forget characters who are human, but who have amassed special powers (e.g., The Shadow, Sherlock Holmes). And what about quasi-human robotic forms, easy to love for their skills and mischievous behaviors (e.g., Minions)?

There is a risk in all this imaginative frivolity. While risk is often ignored, its implications for erasing human identity by collecting, collating, and archiving all information (*sans* actual lived experience of the individual), seeks to create and sustain a detached image of humanity, objectifying existence, seeking control.

Playing with Life: Human Fallibility and Evolution

All of this occurring amidst awe-inspiring and life-enhancing changes, has raises the possibility humans are caught in spectacularly engineered path pushing toward massive changes in views of human nature. The forces seem immutable to our understanding; yet are present and visible to any willing to consider a creative evolutionary idea.

It is my thought there is an evolutionary force for the survival of all life not always evidenced or manifested in human forms at this time. There is a cosmic evolutionary force. Humans, in our quest for greed, power, and control, have abandoned the conditions necessary for human survival by exploiting other life forms, and destroying conditions for life to exist. We are ignoring larger evolutionary purposes inherent in our cosmic creation and consciousness.

Is this an evolutionary imperative? Is evolution playing itself out as a struggle with those with wealth, power, and position to dominate others in some distorted Darwinian or Spenserian scenario? Are the notions of "survival of the fittest" and "biological primacy," taken from original contexts of thought by 19th and 20th Century thinkers to present times, finding themselves accepted and actualized as evolutionary truths? "Survival comes to those capable of surviving by having all resources necessary for survival in a technological age, including mass cloning, frozen embryos, and scores of techniques available to those with wealth, power, and position."

In plain words, amidst the chaos of our times in which extinction of life forms is proceeding recklessly, are they keys to survival available only to those whose resources permit them to continue their lives in altered forms, or perhaps even on new planets?

My deduction from my views on "Lifeism" is human beings are caught in a bio-technical evolution, an unfolding of possibilities leading to extinction of human life (i.e., human nature) as we currently know and define it; we are on a path soon to be dominated by bio-robotic forms. What is at stake is not only humanity, but all forms of existing life. This is the paradox and reality. We benefit from bio-technology advances, and yet they pose a challenge. This the "yes" and "no" (*sic et non*) of our situation.

Some Assumptions

- The "Big Bang" moment of creation was driven by, and embodies, the life impulse innervating all matter and energy, especially via principles of fission (separation) and fusion (connection);

- There is an inherent impulse within our universe and its various life representations, driven by both past forces and events, and yet simultaneously pushed by unfolding future events - a kind of purposive unfolding toward unrealized potentials and possibilities. Is the past prologue? Or is the past being played out toward an existing possible range of outcomes?

- Human beings are only one expression of the life force animating the universe – especially our existing world. Humans are not the "masters" of life; indeed, humans have engaged in destructive influences. But humans possess, although some may question this, a special form of awareness, "consciousness," enabling them to engage in self-reflection or self-reflexive alertness to their experience and behavior.

- Human capabilities for survival, via thought, creativity, and problem solving, have given rise to "advances," now far beyond the structural and monumental developments of civilizations, to the power to alter conventional views of "human nature." "Human is as human does," is a commentary on the emerging developments regarding robotic and mechanical forms.

- It is possible, within this controversial context, an evolution is occurring in "bio-robotic" forms (e.g., android) becoming expressions and manifestations of future human beings.

- This is being achieved through daily developments of new bio-robotic forms and processes. It is likely bio-robotic forms will persist and survive, even as human survival relinquishes (i.e., abandons, yields, gives up) its position, via either force. or an evolutionary process, a process seeking the promotion of life, but not necessarily human life.

Questions:

Are we relinquishing human identity? Are we relinquishing human nature? ... Are we relinquishing nature?

Asian Thought: Unraveling Knots

Reflexive Possibilities of Taoism, Confucianism, Buddhism: Insufficient as Part -- Sufficient as a Whole! And, What of Shintoism? ©

The Nature of "Nothing"

Something cannot come from "nothing," according to rules of logic inherent in accepted denotative and connotative semantic "word" meanings and uses.

"Something" can come from "nothing," however, if the word "nothing" is considered insufficient for understanding the nature of "nothingness." Much as the word "zero" has different meanings and implications among different disciplines (e.g., mathematics, imaginary-space analysis, astrophysics) we can consider various meanings of "nothing" among different ways of knowing.

It is alleged *"zero"* was the creation of Hindu scholars. Zero denotes the absence of any "quantity." Philosophically, however, and from a semantic point of view, can something be nothing? Or is "nothing" merely a word used to express and communicate a bewildering effort to understand and apprehend phenomena.

We must remember the wonders of mathematics "confine" us to rules, premises, and assumptions of internally consistent symbols and numbers. There is beauty, and there is possibility, in mathematics in the hands and minds of geniuses. Mathematics is what mathematics does! In its free use and exploration of an internally consistent system, "nothing" is merely a concept to be explored, and to be used for expanding imaginations of possibility.

"Nothing," after all, is a word! In my opinion, we are captive to conventional meanings of the word "nothing;" there may be value for advancing thought if we move beyond the word "nothing" limitations, and examine how three major flows of Asian thought and religion, may, in fact, be a borderless blend.

Thus, if "nothingness" has a nature unlimited by the inherent logic and meaning of the word "nothing," but "nothingness" can be imagined to assume different natures, including among it "infinity," we have a nature of existing disparate parts seeking to become a harmonious or ordered "something."

And when an appropriate opportunity emerges, then "nothing" meets criteria for both *Taoism* and *Confucianism*. In both of these instances, there is an effort after respecting the endless flow that cannot be known, and the pursuit of a harmonious ordering among disparate parts, endless infinity is "something," not "nothing!"

Further, if we accept "something" can come from "nothing," and it can also return to "nothing," then we can accommodate *Buddhist* notions of the inherent search for conscious -- "oneness, in which "nothingness" and "somethingness" are fused into a "semantic" experiential existence exceeding constraints imposed by language and lived experience. Pursue "emptiness," rid mind of thoughts, and find existence in the vastness of "nothingness."

Accommodating Taoism, Confucianism, and Buddhism

If you are willing to play with this analysis of words, meanings, and possibilities of purposive existence and non-existence, we have an opportunity to (1) grasp *Taoism*, (i.e., the true *Tao* cannot be understood if words are used), and (2) *Confucianism* (i.e., there is an inherent natural effort and impulse toward harmony even in "nothingness, by becoming "something" in a harmony seeking relation and connection).

This also opens possibilities for using language as a tool in the service of meaning-making -- to accommodate *Buddhist* beliefs in "oneness," as being neither "nothing" nor "something," but an emergent quality of meaningful conscious immersion experience from the interaction and experience of both terms.

Shintoism

There remains another major religious orientations and philosophy deserving consideration among the major Asian religious traditions – *Shintoism*. *Shintoism* is Japanese in its origins. *Shintoism* speaks directly to ontological premises and assumptions distinctly Japanese, and yet, assumptions embodying more widespread views about nature and life. Its origins and consequences have implications for a number of topics, from economics, politics, and social formations to aesthetics, all in a "divine" quests for "unity" and "harmony" with nature.

In some ways, *Shintoism* can be positioned above *Confucianism* in a categorical hierarchy, because *Shintoism* transcends explicit rules and guidelines for daily social relations and obligations (e.g., Confucian meritocracy), and positions itself as the origin of the Japanese people as both "part of nature" and as "nature."

For me, this acknowledges the recognition of life itself, as a creative force animating the universe. It goes beyond privileging human life as being apart from all life. The notion of "mankind as master," has proven to be a serious problem in which accepted human dominance has led to dramatic, but pernicious, changes

Lifeism

I proposed the concept of *"Lifeism,"* as going beyond humanism, so humanity can grasp the deeper meanings and purposes of human existence within the larger life impulse inherent in all living things – fission and fusion of all things from the earliest moment of creation (i.e., big bang). The entire cosmos is alive – we should not be misled by restricted ideas and notions of life offered by those who choose to define "life" in a limited way. Life abounds throughout our world in different forms of existence and manifestation, all animated by a life impulse.

Consider the possibility "consciousness" itself, is a state of being in the world and the cosmos – a state in which all things have a sentient awareness. This is not always apparent to us, but implies relationship to other things, especially those things most immediately in its presence. In other words, there is an effort after survival and recreation in all things, drawing upon those immediate circumstances and situations in which it is embedded -- a magnificent ecology of embedded relations in which each "part" actually exists within itself, and also within a context, yielding "awareness."

The failure of our thinking regarding "consciousness" is we assign "consciousness" as a property of the brain, and not mind! Mind is the broader awareness, responsiveness, to the milieu in which something exists. The brain is a vehicle enabling this awareness, the mechanism. Mind is existence in context! Mind is the emergent phenomena of brain in context.

All living things have sentient mechanisms. It is essential we recognize "NOTHING" exists apart from anything else. Even being placed in vacuum, would constitute a new milieu of existence. Context is our milieu interacting with an organism (i.e., object). Each organism, no matter how small or large, responds to the milieu in an effort after survival.

For human beings, efforts after survival involve a search for meaning, for meaning making! There are endless numbers of shared meanings, encoded as philosophies, religions, and various belief and life style systems.

Consciousness in its "awareness" expression is a life-endowed property; all things created from the moment of the "Big Bang," have that property. What is critical here is the recognition of relationship (e.g., ecology, interdependency, connection, bond, union, attachment, linkage). This then is the nature of consciousness: an emergent property of all things, in which "connection," perhaps even optimal "connection," is present in and for survival, growth, and development.

This assumes we recognize and acknowledge in all things expressing, manifesting, and evidencing life, (and those we do not), the potential to become a number of other expressions and evidencing, actualizing the possibilities.

Our dilemma, as human beings, is we have restricted notions of human nature, and limited notions of "life," especially "life's" nature, as the expression or manifestation of purposes and endless possibilities. The biggest secret or mystery is not human purpose and meaning, but life's purpose and meaning.

For me, this secret is an unfolding of endless and unknown potential. Even when we use natural resources as sources of energy, we become confined to thinking of coal and oil as energy commodities and substances. They are so much more! They reflect life's multitude of properties – the capacity to become other than what may be immediately apparent.

Humans are part of life, not masters of life. Answers to profound questions are to be found in acknowledging this fact! The great religions and philosophies are human creations responding to inherent impulses of all life to evidence itself and to evolve. The separation of ideas and the connection of ideas yield potential insights for human understanding.

Our human problem is our limited vision and infatuation with self, and the words and moral thought systems we have created as templates. They are, in fact, templates, but we see them as absolutes. Each template has a range of convenience, a limited latitude for revealing and securing insights.

We seek, as human beings, special states of being, or non-being, like the states of awaking and enlightenment described in *Sartori* and *Nirvana.* In these states there is an awareness of *"self,"* and with it a cosmic-like ascent into "nothingness" that must be pursued until such time "nothingness" becomes "pure" awareness.

It is almost as if all the boundaries of human existence and experience, defined by energy, matter, gravity and magnetism, are escaped. We are now in a quantum state of chance particle motions and relations. We are "something," and we are "nothing."

We exist for brief moments, only to lose existence, and to recover it again and again. Higgs-Boson particles! Higgs-Boson processes? Dark matter! Dark energy! We experience and pursue transformations of "nothing" into "something," and "something" into "nothing!" A way of escaping "being," unfettered by order and presence! We are in constant creation, and we also depart creation, simultaneously. It is paradox! But it is only paradoxical if we prize and adhere to one way of thinking.

And So . . . ?

This brings us back to *Buddhism, Confucianism, Taoism,* and *Shintoism.* They are separate, but they are the same when language and words are understood beyond accepted denotative and connotative meanings. They are the same when we enter the realm of ambiguous meanings, and transcendent spiritual experiences. They merge into one another, reflecting dimensions of larger meaning. That is their magnificence! They are guides for evolving, unfolding, becoming, and entering horizons of possibility for experiences no longer confined to the ordinary.

Yes, yes, I know! I can hear the critiques! Readers shocked at my audacity! My efforts to address the impossible! My willingness to write of things unknown to me, and yet known to me! But isn't it fun! Isn't is okay to try, to explore ideas within the limits of your knowledge, even when you know the products of your thought may be subject to rejection. I think so! I am so! So what?

Lifeism: Beyond Humanity

The Cosmos and Us

As we seek answers to important questions of life -- meaning, purpose, existence, and identity -- we too often ignore or forget one of the most obvious sources of insight for our being -- the act of cosmic creation -- that moment known affectionately -- and incorrectly -- as the "Big Bang Theory."

Although astrophysicists are mindful of this critical moment, seeking to understand its origins and consequences, there are too few commentators who find philosophical, theological, and psychological, significance in this moment. How often do we seek answers to what we are, who we are, and what we are becoming within that very moment in which creation of the universe occurred?

It is assumed, and evidence mounts daily, there was enormous explosion of a single infinitesimally small mass or concentration of matter/energy hurled in a billionth of a second across the space/time of our cosmos. This moment lead to the formations of our galaxy with its billions of stars, the Milky Way Galaxy, and of billions of other galaxies extending to a current accepted "known" distance of 14.5 -- 14.7 billion lights years.

And now as if to make humans seem even more infinitesimally small and inconsequential, astrophysicists are speaking of universes beyond our universe, and of an endless dance of creation in which there is a constant process of "fission" (separation) and "fusion" (connection). Fission and fusion are at the heart of our universe as we know it. Energy, matter, dark matter, gravity, space, time, black holes, quasars are the stuff of our universe. And everywhere, amidst this cosmic wonder, we can see the processes of separation and connection.

For me, there are important insights for us as human beings regarding our popular perceptions of human nature, and our failure to grasp fission and fusion, separation and connection, diversity and unity, part and whole, abstractions in physics, apply to us! At the core of this thought is the concept of context. All things exist in context! By context I mean the notable relationships (some would say "ecology") bringing with them changes associated with survival, growth, and development. I believe humans have lost their sense of place in our universal contextual order.

Learning from a Weed

What is important in these remarks are the implications they have had for my embracing the act of "cosmic creation" as a powerful idea for bringing together three interesting topics regarding context: "Life," "Humanism," and "Hope." I stumbled across this view of "connection" by accident.

It was a hot day in the city of Atlanta, Georgia, where I live. And I was traveling to town only to be caught in a huge traffic jam on the major highway. The traffic was brought to a standstill, and after the usual blaring of horns, expressions of irritation, and collection of noxious fumes in the heat of day, I simply turned off my ignition, pulled down the window, and decided to wait it out. There is a certain comfort in accepting one's fate when it is clear that no amount of struggle will yield a change.

As I looked out the car window at the long concrete barrier separating different streams of driving, I noticed a small clump of green weeds pushing up between a slight crevice in the concrete. There, amidst the oppressive heat, the noxious fumes, noise, and the absence of any substantial amount of earth and water, there emerged a small clump of green weeds. Do you grasp that image? Life was rearing itself under the harshest of conditions. Life would not be denied.

There was no question of preference or choice of locations by this small weed, there was only its intent to grow, and to become what it was capable of becoming within the limited context it had been given. It was driven by life itself, the force that animates the universe, and all about us, and pursuing an evolutionary course of becoming in its manifestations, all it is capable of being.

The automobile traffic began to flow once again, and I was forced to drive away from this green weed giving me so much insight. But I took with me the image of the moment as an understanding of the mystery of life itself — its omnipresence, its omnipotence, its absolute capacity to exist in a myriad of ways, forms, and expressions inherent within it seed and sanctioned by its milieu. I understood in those few moments a number of things about life, purpose, and meaning. The Germans call this type of immediate insight and apprehending, *Verstehen*, *meaning* sudden insightful learning across the totality of being, by the totality of being.

Assigning human qualities to nonhuman forms of life is questionable, unless one considers are common origins. I kept wondering to myself if "hope" in humans is related to a felt sense that even under the precarious conditions in which sub-human and non-human life forms may find themselves in at any given moment, there is the potential to realize survival, growth, and development – change!

Is the human experience of "hope" a response to the amazing forces of life to endure amidst adversity? Is "hope" the resonance or echo of the push and pull to survive amidst difficult circumstances? Is the awareness of "distinction" (i.e., part) somehow also an awareness of the opportunity for connection and restoration of a fulfilling context? Is the life force within all of us, and within all living things, a powerful residue of that moment in cosmic creation when all became separate and yet connected?

Life as "Potential"

The concept of "potential" is important here. Potential is an inherent fundamental characteristic of life. Munroe (2007) described potential in this way:

> Potential is dormant ability, reserved power, untapped strength, unused success, hidden talents, capped culpability... All you can be but have not yet become, all you can do but have not yet done, how far you can reach, but have not yet reached, what you can accomplish but have not yet accomplished. Potential is unexposed ability and latent power (Munroe, 2007: 3). Munroe is referring to human potential, but his words reveal a great deal about the potential of life itself. For isn't there present in each seed or spore of life, the capability to become all that it can be within the constraints of its milieu? Isn't life itself a seemingly endless potential to become varied, diverse, and fulfilled in al of its capabilities?

> Using the metaphor of the seed, Munroe (2007), states: If I held a seed in my hand and asked you, "What do I have in my hand"?" What would you say: "a seed!" However, if you understand the nature of the seed, your answer would be fact, but not truth. The truth is I hold a forest in my hand. Why? Because in every seed see there is a tree, and in every tree there is fruit or flowers with seed in them. . . . In essence what you see is not all there is. That is potential. Not what is, but what could be (Munroe, 2007: 1).

This is what I believe we are failing to grasp. This is what is limiting our identity and responsibility. As we proceed recklessly toward of down a path of killing and destruction, we are failing to identify with life. We are destroying not only human lives, but life itself. It is insufficient for us to address the problems before us with humanistic and humanitarian efforts, important as these may be. We must move beyond our pre-occupation and prioritization with humanity, and placed ourselves within the larger context of life. That is our true identity!

Identity: Separation and Connection

The emergence of a global era, a borderless psychological and physical milieu, confronts us with new and bewildering challenges to identity formation, change, and assertion. Age-old questions regarding identity: "Who am I?" What do I believe?" "What is my purpose?" "What are my responsibilities?" "How did I become who I am?" must be answered amidst a context of unavoidable competing and conflicting global forces giving rise to increasing levels of uncertainty, unpredictability, confusion, and fear. Indeed, many of our traditional political, economic, social, and religious institutions, long major sources for shaping individual and collective identities, have become part of the problems we face in identity formation and negotiation.

We have as humans abandoned our responsibilities, duties, and obligations to life itself. Placing other identities (e.g., personal, familial, ethnic, racial, national) before our most basic one. We are above all, children of the cosmos, products of fission and fusion, products of forces engrained in every cell in our body, and of that special gift of "mind." Mind arises, not from brain, but from the ecology of person and setting in which we are all embedded. It is mind, not brain, giving us choice. It is mind, not brain, giving us meaning and purpose.

Mind, then, is an emergent property of being that responds not to our isolated bodies, to our separation, but to our relations with the larger contexts in which we are embedded. And it is here, I believe, covenants, contracts, and promises with gods led us astray. Today those aspects of our lives are causing much destruction and suffering. There is no "other," and this is what you recognize and share by your work. We do good not because we fear an angry god, but because love, compassion, and empathy are inherent in our being, because they promote life.

Amidst the very "explosive" nature of our universe, within especially the black holes of collapse and rebirth at their center; there is, if we choose to see it, a delicate cosmic dance in which creation, renewal, and resurrection are present. It is too distant for our now dulled senses to grasp, appreciate, and respond to with the humility and awe that should be present.

Personal, Cultural, and National Identities

A sense of identity is at the core of human existence and meaning. It is the self-reflective and dialogical anchor, both conscious and unconscious, grounding us amidst the constant flow of changes in our settings and situations. It offers us a sense of who we are and what we are. The many and varied forces that shape our identity(s) are determined by both unique and shared experiences. The accumulation of these lived experiences, their dynamic interactions and their constant appraisal, evaluation, and modifications, form the crucible in which we, as individuals and members of groups, claim place, position, and agency.

Human beings have many different identities, including personal, cultural, and national identities. Each of these identities commands loyalties since they define and position self. At a personal level, identity can be a source of great comfort or a source of great conflict and difficulty. This is very clear in adolescence when a youth is forming an identity, a process that continues through a lifetime. At a cultural level, identities enable us to function within boundaries of acceptability and deviance according to various norms accepted through socialization. Similarly, at a national level (see Footnote A at end of paper), our identification with a nation can lead to excessive nationalism, and a willingness to fight and/or die for our country. Erich Fromm (1955), a social psychoanalyst, stated this very well:

> The problem of the sense of identity is not, as it is usually understood, merely a philosophical problem, or a problem only concerning our mind and thought. The need to feel a sense of identity stems from the very condition of human existence, and it is the source of the most intense strivings. Since I cannot remain sane without the sense of "I," I am driven to do almost anything to acquire this sense. Behind the intense

passion for status and conformity is this very need, and it is sometimes even stronger than the need for physical survival. What could be more obvious than the fact that people are willing to risk their lives, to give up their love, to surrender their freedom, to sacrifice their own thoughts, for the sake of being one of the herd, of conforming, and thus of acquiring a sense of identity, even though it is an illusory one (Fromm, 1955, p. 63).

But amidst this quest for identity, essential to human functioning, we are missing an identification that may be critical for our survival, and that is an identity with life itself. We seem oblivious to the fact that above all things, we are alive, and life deserves our loyalty as much as any other identity we may have or pursue. We are more than humanity, and we must identify ourselves with more than humanity. We are embedded in life; we are surrounded and immersed in life in millions of ways. It is the most obvious and yet most ignored aspect of our being, and in our ignorance, we fail to see that we are connected, united, linked to so much more beyond ourselves. And that "connection" holds the key to our very nature.

Yet, we find ourselves as human beings assaulting and killing life in all its forms, species are becoming extinct, bio-diversity is declining, global warming is occurring, and there is a depletion of our water, energy, and agricultural resources, and wars and conflict are endemic.

I suggest a solution for many of the challenges we face may be to move beyond our conventional identifications with self, culture, nation, and even humanity, to identification with life -- **Lifeism.**

Lifeism encourages us to encounter and to reflect on death, and to understand its inseparable relation to life. As we behold life in all of its forms, as we witness its blossoming and its passing, we become acutely aware of the inevitable cycle of life and death, especially the reality life and death are one! To understand and to accept the mystery that life and death are one enriches our life, and promotes a greater sense of responsibility to support life in all forms. **Life and death are one!**

References

Fromm, E. (1955). *The sane society.* New York: Henry Holt.
Munroe, Myles (2007). *Devotional Journal.* Shippensburg, PA: Destiny Image Publishers.

Imprints of Time and Place

- Return to the Church
  of Santa Margherita
- Quaker Meeting:
  People Come into Our Lives… Jacob
- "Thinking about Georgia…
  Thoughts on My Mind"
- Paris Past: The Last Time I Saw…

Return to the Church Of Santa Margherita

My heart trembles as I cross the cobblestone street
    To the Church of Santa Margherita.

I enter through ancient wrought iron gates,
    As once we did so long ago,
        Pausing to see what time has changed.

I pray everything will be as it was then.
    Years have passed in grief and longing,
        Much as we said they would.

I still yearn for your touch,
    Begging destiny to bring us together,
        Pleading with fate for the sight of your face,
            Bargaining with God!

I walk the wet-clay path to the Church doors,
    Passing tombs of century-old icons:
        Writers and warriors,
            Sinners and saints!

The path is marked by footprints of others,
    Temporary imprints,
        To be erased by wind and rain.

It is noon, as it was then,
    The sky is blue, unsullied by clouds.
        The magpies too are there:
            "Messengers of the gods," you said.

II.

I open century-old doors,
    Heavy with iron clasps,
        Weathered and worn.
           I enter my past.

The altar looms in the distance
    Neath a score of vaulted arches,
        Each a haven for Biblical myths!

Sunlight streams through Gothic windows,
    Bathing white-plaster walls in solar purity.

High above ordered wooden pews,
    Hangs an ornate gold pulpit.

I search for the vaulted arch of John IV:
    The Good Samaritan!
        It was here we sat.

"Whoever drinks the water, I give him
    Will never thirst.
        I who speak to you, am he."

I sit in Row 10, alone,
    A single penitent
        Kneeling at the altar pew,
           Waiting . . . .

Tears flood my eyes,
    Streaming across my face,
        A litany of memories!

Auburn hair! Auburn hair!
Translucent skin!
Velvet voice: Soft, breathless;

Brown eyes:
Alive, passionate.
Radiant coals in a darkened peasant hut.

Was it a dream?
    Were you an apparition?
        An archetypal image of a saint,
            Princess from days of seers and magicians;
                An ethereal vision spun by an entranced mind.

Did I create you?
    Did I seek union with my past?
        Or were you real?
            A reincarnation of all I have sought for centuries,
              A grail rekindling flames of unrequited love.

A painting of crucified Christ overwhelms the altar below:
    Nothing has changed . . . but time.

Comment:

I wrote the first words of this poem in 1987. Through the years, I changed the words a score of times, each time reliving a moment in time that was for me momentous in its release from the life I had known. Less anyone wonder, nothing ever happened from the meeting with this woman in the *Church of Santa Margharita.* It is true there was a special magic, but only a held hand and smile; it was never consummated. It was as if both knew doing more would break the spell that had been cast. From this meeting, a flood of poems would arise. My emotions were freed. I could write!

Quaker Meeting:
People Come into Our Lives . . . Jacob

I.

People enter our lives at unexpected times,
    Changing us in profound ways . . .
        A glance, a smile or frown,
            A word -- spoken or written --
                An act of kindness or harm!

Some remain in our lives for a lifetime,
    Others for a moment!
        Whatever it may be,
            The entry of "others" into our lives
                Is always an encounter of consequence!
                    It should not to be treated lightly,
                Nor dismissed as chance!

The entry into our lives of "others"
    Is to be pursued -- explored, understood,
        For it is more than it seems,
            It is a sealing of minds, lives, and spirits.
            It is a connection.

II.

I was blessed yesterday to meet a man
    -- A person of color –
        A man of quiet dignity,
            His years honed by life lived amidst

Doubts and uncertainties,
Unanswered questions,
A man -- humble and sincere!

I listened as he spoke of his life.
Not a frozen written narrative,
But an unfolding of his heart!
Graceful words,
Magnified in meaning
By the deliberate meter of his speech!
A sacred moment!

The man spoke of his lifetime search -- his longing
For a home -- not a house -- but a home --
A place, anchor, refuge . . . for his soul!
A grounded piece of earth,
Upon which he could stand,
Plant roots, grow, and become.
A place where he could say:
"I am home."

III.

I was changed by his words.
He may never know this
Unless along the way,
He finds this poem.
But no more needs to be said.

I will remember his lined face,
Gentle voice,
Deep set eyes,
Peaceful countenance . . .
All shaping the moment,
Affirming -- forever --
There is no "other."
Thank you, Jacob.

I wrote this poem on October 29, 2012, following my attendance at a Quaker Meeting in Decatur, Georgia. At the meeting, several Quakers spoke of the course of their involvement in the Quaker way-of-life. One of the speakers was an African American middle-aged man. The sincerity of his words remained with me. I came home and wrote the poem amidst memories of his speaking. I was captivated by his purity -- his grace amidst a lifetime of hardship approached being sacred

"Thinking About Georgia . . . Thoughts on My Mind"
(A Fictional Story)

Prelude

When Ray Charles sings "Georgia on My Mind," listeners are captivated by the words and music -- his plaintive longing for a land and place of special meaning and attachment. His longing resonates as he sings with his throaty raspy tones, and poignant pauses. For many born and raised in Georgia, the song brings more than a flood of feelings and memories; it is a reminder of their life, their way-of-being -- a deep awareness they cannot escape Georgia, with all its calls and ties. Georgia is inscribed in their mind and heart, it is a collage of images, sounds, and smells unique to the land and people.

This is a short story about one person among many from Georgia -- a young hair stylist, Cassandra, born and reared in rural Georgia. The story grew from a brief conversation – I had with Cassandra -- more like a narrative, since all I did was listen and nod. Within the span of time of a slow haircut, undisturbed by a lack of customers, Cassandra wove her life story, bringing home for me the reality of the lives behind the people we interact with each day as we shop and follow our daily routines. Lives filled with the richness of life itself – its enchantments and its sorrows, lives we miss sharing, as we proceed with daily routines isolating us from one another, turning each encounter into a brief exchange of goods and services, even in families, if the latter still exist.

I learned a life lesson that day about the importance of understanding the deep experiences characterizing all our lives, experiences often hidden, or passed over and dismissed as inconsequential or an unnecessary addition to minds already over burdened with thoughts, obligations, responsibilities. Life moves fast today in our consumer culture with its daily list of things to be done or accomplished. Our lives have become scorecards in which winning or losing days depend on the final summary of tasks completed or missed.

It was not like that in Georgia, and in so many other places as well. I don't wish to romanticize the past, because there is so much to regret for so many, especially African-Americans whose lives were fixed in a rigid status order limiting their opportunities, imposing a painful burden of daily fear. But amidst past times, people seemed to matter more, especially in the ordered life of small towns in Georgia. Rich or poor, Black or white, our involvement was more than a commercial exchange.

For better or for worse, people knew one another, or tried to know one another, and understood the need to get along, and to respond with some degree of civility and gentility. There is always the gap between the ideal and the real, but the ideal was pursued, and the real was tolerated, but always real was considered.

We don't attend to the people today, even as we exchange brief and reflexive pleasantries: "How yah doing today, sir?" *"Well, I'm thankful I made it through the night."* "That'll be $8.95, sir." "Have a blessed day." *"You have one too."*

Meeting Cassandra

I met Cassandra in a corporate-franchised hair-style shop. All shops are dominated by color combinations of Georgia's proud winning football teams, either the iconic red and black of the University of Georgia "Dawgs," or the gold and black of the Georgia Tech "Rambling Wreck." Both universities have been national champions in college football. The up and down moods of Georgia residents are often a function of the fortunes of these two storied teams. Football is king! In Georgia, football on Friday night is for high schools, on Saturday afternoon for colleges, and on Sunday noon for the Atlanta Falcons, a professional football team whose popular team cheer is: "Rise Up." "Rise Up" . . . sounds like a remnant cry of the Civil War

In Georgia, of course, you are never quite sure if they are referring to the South, or to the Falcons football team, since many Georgians refuse to believe the South was defeated in the Civil War. But that is only an aside comment. Just something I observed from living her twelve years. Let me get back to Cassandra, and to what she taught me. A slow business day afforded her an opportunity to share her life story, and it gave me a chance to learn a life lesson about the importance of connections among people.

My words do not do justice to Cassandra. There is so much more I would like to know, and to write about her. Unfortunately, when I returned for another hair cut three weeks later, she was no longer employed at the shop, and no one would tell me where she had gone. Her natural and unaffected way-of-talking about her life, her willingness to share private thoughts and observations, and her choice to speak to me so openly, left me captivated by her person, and left me a better person. She may never know she helped me understand Georgia, people, and life itself, a little better than the day I entered the shop, expecting only a haircut.

Cassandra

Cassandra was 25 years old -- spoke with a rural small-town Georgia twang and drawl. She had a near-constant smile on her face -- a gentle smile -- that said much about her nature and temperament. She said, **"Welcum,"** as I walked into the shop. And when she said, **"Welcum,"** you knew she meant it. I think it was impossible for her to hide her feelings from herself or from others. She had no frills, no unnecessary charms -- just a rural Georgia girl, whose charm resides in her transparency.

Cassandra wasn't trying to be anything other than her self. She needed no religion to guide her life, although being a Baptist or a non-denominational Christian in Georgia is the norm. Encounters sometimes begin or end with "Praise the Lord," or "God is great." Cassandra was good by nature and temperament, in spite of life experiences warranting a dampened, sullied, contained style.

"My name's Cassandra. Y'all can call me Cass. I'll be with yah in sec. Take that chair ovuh there. Just let me get this hair on the floor swept up. That last guy could have sold his hair downtown for money – it was sooo long."

Cassandra grinned at me; her face lit up with a slight blush – she knew she wasn't supposed to say something about customers, especially when the manager, was watching on the security camera in the back room. She looked at my short-white thinning hair and laughed: **"Well y'ah got nothin to sell downtown."**

Cassandra was quick with her words. Obviously intelligent -- a high school graduate, who probably got by in school by doing what was needed, and not too much more. In the course of my haircut, I came to see Cassandra as a "rebel without a cause" -- a person out of place in her time and yet caught in it. She was just trying to survive. Just trying to make sense about her life – growing up in a small-town rural Georgia amidst a family filled with discord and want.

She accepted things were the way they were, but always kept wondering in the back of her mind, if there was something more to it all. If there was any reason to hope things could be better, or if they were fixed, and set in motion long ago, as if by some Calvinistic force.

There is no doubt in my mind Cassandra is hoping the forces of fate have not sealed her life. I could sense a quiet desperation in her as she spoke to me. I wondered whether she was sharing her life in an openness hoping it might just result in some new opportunity for her. She wasn't looking for happiness. I think fulfillment is a better word: be someone, fit in somewhere, find a little comfort, find some certainty, and most of all, make sense of all that happened to her as she grew up in rural Georgia.

I listened to Cassandra's life narrative unfold in plain direct words; words whose meaning were enhanced by her lilt, pace, and unassuming insight and wisdom. She was not a world traveler whose life was filled with many experiences, but the experiences she accumulated in her young life were not to be dismissed as unimportant. They were her experiences, and she had given them richness because they defined her identity, what she believed, what she hoped, and who she was.

I thought back to my own youth and the "folk song" era of the early sixties -- black jeans, turtle neck sweater, cigarette, small water glass of *Mateus* wine -- people talking about life, meaning, purposes. And when the bottle was drained, you used it for a dripping candle holder . . . its unique oval shape: Simple beauty!

In that era, it was as if the world was coming out of the calm and convention of the Eisenhower years; we were testing new limits, sometimes breaking old ones for the sheer delight of surprise on the faces of the older folks of the "best generation." There was, in the emerging era, an openness fueled by the very songs themselves: "How many roads must a man walk down, before they call him a man . . . ?" But most of all, there was trust in friends, a shared sense of searching for identity, of exploring self beyond the fixed identity one had been given by circumstance.

As the minutes of the haircut passed, I learned more about Cassandra's youth – her hopes, her dreams. Cassandra was especially eager to talk when I told her I was a psychologist. **"Oh, that was mah favorite subject in high school. Learning all about why we act like we do. Ah loved it."** Cassandra liked her job, not the standing for hours cutting hair, sweeping floors, and waiting for customers, but the chance to meet new people, talking with customers, and talking story with the other girls in the shop, hearing their life experiences, sharing an experience vicariously with a quick phrase – **"For real!"**

Cassandra was good at what she did, and she knew it. That brought her some satisfaction in her otherwise routine day. She wanted more, but I learned she had been beaten down along the way, and had learned to not want too much, if only to prevent disappointment. She was versed in down-home wisdom and homilies: **"Y'ah jest got to take what is on your plate, and make the most of it. Sometime the ribs are bettah than other times; may even have some meat on em."**

Smile! Quick words to comfort and soothe troubled times. But her words were also something more. They were telling me something about her. She wanted me to know her, to see her as a person, a Georgia girl, and so much more.

Cassandra had cut my hair the last time I went to the shop – best haircut I had in years. But it was a quick 1-2-3 haircut. **"Hi! Welcum! How yah doin? What sort of cut do yah want?** The shop was filled with customers during my last visit, and there were quotas to be filled. I remembered her because she was cheery, cute, a buoyant spirit -- long dark hair, dark eyes, a pearl beneath her lip, another on her eyelid, small pierced pearl earrings, her name and tattoos of swirling designs on both arms. But most of all, she had an inner presence! It radiated! It was undeniable!

I also recalled Cassandra wore a large digital black watch on her left wrist displaying the time in visible bold-black numerals. Time was important for her. Later, when I came home, I understood time had always been important for her, she was waiting for life to happen, and she knew she did not have forever.

"Heck, aah'm 25 years old. Most ah the girls I know are married and have kids already. I am behind. Don't know if thah happy, but at least thah doing what thah was expected to do."

This comment was accompanied by quick grin and laugh. Cassandra was waiting, trying to make sense of it all amid a history of want, routine, and abuse. In my first visit to the shop, brief as it was, she had told me all she wanted was . . . **"A good man, a house, and some kids. A place to plant roots! I love family, but mine leaves much to be desired. Don't want to make the same mahstakes."**

"Business seems slow," I said, as I eased into the padded swivel chair, placing my IPhone and glasses on the shelf.

"Yeah, we got to start marketin this place. Not sure it's the best location," she replied.

"Yah know what we ought to do? We ought to get a contract to cut hair over at the old folks' home. There are three homes within a mile. Lotsa old folks just wanted to stay where they are, and not have to get some bus to drive them somewhere."

She smiled, hunched her shoulders, raised her eyebrows, almost as if she wasn't supposed to be thinking like that, just keep her ideas to herself, and do not offer an opinion.

Whenever Cassandra made a comment beyond her expected or conventional role of expertise, cutting hair, she would apologize by hunching her shoulders up, burying her neck, and leaving the words behind with raised eyebrows, a tilt of the head to show her guilt, and a slight glance at my response.

I was glad she was available when I came in the second time. I had forgotten her name, but remembered her face and skills. I was hoping to see her again. This time, fortunately, the shop was totally empty. Unusual! I felt a bit uncomfortable! Hope this was not a set-up. I wondered.

Cassandra had time for talking, and she loved making comments as she walked to different sides of the chair, standing back, looking to see what needed to be cut, adjusting the scissors on her shelf, fixing the towels, a skilled multi-tasker, doing a dozen things within a few seconds.

"Now then, what y'ah wantin today?"

All of this was going on as she looked in the mirror at my head popping up from a black cape, taking in all my face and head could offer her in terms of who I was, what she had to do to cut my hair, and what she could expect in talk from me.

An Unfolding Narrative:

"Did you tell me where you were from the last time? I can tell y'ah a Yankee. Nothing wrong with that; some people down here are still fighting Sherman. I'm not. It is what it is. Don't go makin more trouble for yourself by fighting old battles and wars.

Gun collectors, *'Gone with the Wind,"* and beer just keep things alive here in Georgia. Y'ah would think we are still fighting to save Atlanta. Y'ah see the movie?"

"I heah Margaret Mitchell was really special. Kind of a rebel! Did the unexpected, and got away with it. She's like a saint down heah."

I smile and replied: "Make it close on the side, and don't cut too much off the top. Need all the hair I got left."

"Oh y'ah got good hair. Doncha worry none, hon. I know just the way you want it. Aren't you the "shrink?" I cut your hair the last time you were heah." Well, I could tell you a bit about life."

And she did! I was surprised when Cassandra started talking about her life to me -- her roots, youth, family, small town -- a spontaneous litany of people and events that marked her years, never to be removed or denied. She kept it all inside. She wasn't going to bury or run from what had happened to her. This was her story, and she shared it easily as she cut my hair, a steady, quick-flowing stream of words, followed by brief pauses to check out what needed to be done with a quick flick of the scissors.

Casssandra began by tugging up her salon slacks reflexively. The work uniform: black-stripped exercise slacks, black striped t-shirt top, and a thin necklace. -- black everywhere -- with an occasional touch of red or gold to please all sides -- black walls, towels, chairs, and cabinets. No getting away from where you are -- Georgia, and proud of it.

"**Jawgiah!**" I can't say it the way people raised here say it. It isn't a harsh sound, more like a gentle flow -- emphasis on the second syllable, and then a quiet finish, just like Ray Charles sings it.

I could see a dozen of Cassandra's tattoos -- her name and winding tattoos on left forearm. I am sure she had other tattoos that were hidden -- it was part of the rural life-style to adorn your body with symbols and words that told others who you were, and what someone could expect, even if you were bare-butt naked. No extras -- no surprises. Here's my message! This is who I am.

Small-Town Georgia:

"**See, Ah was born in Mapleville. That's bout 60 miles from heah. Bet y'ah never been there. No reason. Ain't no reason for the folks there, to be there,**" said with a wry smile on her face.

And then Cassandra began to share her story -- her complex, sullied, and brave life story -- a story filled with events, people, and forces you never imagine when you first meet someone, and you reach decisions quickly about who they are, and what you can expect. Case closed! Part of today's life style. Don't get involved. Don't be asking questions about anyone.

Cassandra continued to speak: "**Don't know why they called the town that, since most of trees we have are Georgia Pines. We mustah had some maple trees back a few hundred years. They probably cut them down for lumber. That's Mapleville, cutting down the good stuff, for all the wrong reasons. Nevah thinking ahead**"

"I spent my whole life in that place. Left a few years ago! Had to escape or go mad. Y'all want to know what its like. You're not from Jawgiah. I'll tell yah."

"See everyone knows everyone. Can't do a thing without it comin back to haunt yah. Yah parents know what happened at school before you even get home to tell them. Mah Daddy got hurt bad at the mill, and couldn't work anymore. He's home all the time. Collects a small disabilitah check! My Mom works at the town restaurant – Dottie's Place."

Actually the owner's name was Susan Belle Smith, but she bought it from Dorothy Englander. That's where the name Dottie came from. Cost too much to change the sign in the window – foods the same, so are the tables and chairs. Typical small town! Chicken and dumplins, their best dish. Got a black lady, Momma Jones, cookin in the back, she's been thah for years. Hamburgs, fries, fried chicken, grits, greens, soups, apple pie.

"Mom don't make much in tips unless a team's in town on Friday to play Mapleville. People come to eat thah before the game. We was called the Mapleville Tigers. But our team was more like pussycats; nevah won much.

The guys from the other towns used to say, "All y'all's guys ain't much on the field, but yah cheerleaders are sweet as maple syrup."

She shook her head in disbelief at her very words. **"Can yah believe it?"**

"Y'ah know! Small-town rivalries! Lotta jokes! But deep down, its serious stuff. We make a football game seem like it's the most important thing in the world. People dying all over the place – we're just thinking whether we goin win or lose by a touchdown."

"My brothuh, Earl, played football a few years back. Now he just relives those days. All he can talk bout. He gets a couple beers in him, and starts rememberin. Same story, same words, nevah changes."

FRIDAY NIGHT FOOTBALL:

"Hey, Cass, remembuh when we beat Zebulon. Hell! That was some game. I remember that game more than any othah. I had to square off against a big black guy cross the line, and he was kickin mah white ass. He outweighed me by 50 pounds. Coach called a time out, and takes me and Pinto aside, -- you remember Pinto, doncha, Cass? He was part Cherokee, and part elephant."

"Anyway, coach sez to me and Pinto: Hey, you two candy asses. That's all y'ah are! Pieces of candy for a black man! I'm given yah one chance before I put freshman in to embarrass your dumb asses. So, on the next play ... Pinto, let him in then chop his legs. Earl you fall hard on him! Knock the wind out of him. Got it? Now show me somethin, or warm your butts on the bench. Low and high! High and low! Do it"

"Shit, Cass! I felt like I was reborn. I had just been given the gospel. I went back in and told that big bastard across from me: 'C'mon, come get me, cause y'ah a'int nothin but chocolate puddin. C'mon.' I see he's fired up. He gets low and gets to growlin. Comes chargin in like a train."

"Pinto hit him low. I let him fall flat, and then buried my elbow on his back kidney. I could hear him moan. Ref missed the whole thing. That Black bastard was nevuh the same. He was in pain." We lost by a touchdown. But it was sum game, Cass. It was sum game."

I suspect Cass heard the story so many times she could tell it back to Earl word for word – and he would have loved it. But she listened to him, because she knew it was important to him. And that's who she was. She was there to care for the family. Bad as her family life was, she was there for them -- they were her family.

Cass had just the right inflections when she was sharing the story with me. You could almost see Earl standing there – sweat on his face, grass stains on his jersey, eyes glazed, puffing and heavin, helmet in hand. Friday-night football in Georgia! Holy Wars!

"My brothuh is still the same as he was then. Never grew up. No job. Just a dreamer! Stays at home! Helps my Daddy move around! They drink a few beers, and watch TV all day and night. Nothin else to do! Earl dates a gal from his class. They just sit at the bar, get a buzz, and then, yah know, go over to her place."

"I asked my momma and daddy why do we stay heah? They jest looked at me kind of simple, and said: This is our home! This is our family's home. This is our land. We all been heah since way back. Your grandpa and grandma were raised heah . . . so was their folks, going back before the Civil War. Jest Scotch-Irish blood . . . came ovah long ago lookin for a new life, and they found it heah. This is our home, Cassandra."

INITIATION:

"I dated a few guys from other towns, but that was frowned on at school. The guys would say: You're Maple ... stick with Maple guys. You can't trust those other guys. Yeah, well, I learned the hard way. You can't trust guys from any town. Thah all the same! No offense." She smiled, hunched her shoulders, raised her eyebrows.

"Got talked into drinking some beer one night, doing some grass, passed out. Got raped.

Cassandra paused here. You could see her mind going back across time, reliving the whole thing. I could see her face in the mirror. She swallowed. Then she got back to talking.

"Ah woke up . . . in an old motel in the next town ovah, clothes all messed up and torn. I hurt so bad down below. Don't know what happened. I know one of the guys who did it to me, because he smiled and winked at me in school a few days later. I was with him that night. I know it was him."

"I told the pahlice. Ha! Yah know what they said: 'Miss, you shouldn't be drinkin and smoking, and expect nuthin's going to happen. Now, unless you got absolute proof, I can't do nothin. I'm sorry.' "So much for the paaahhlice."

"I nevah went to the hospital. I should've, but I was confused, and felt guilty – like it was mah fault. I wasn't a virgin, but I wasn't a bad girl. I'd like to kill him. What he did to me was wrong. I trusted him."

"Hold on!" "Let me tighten your collar a bit, or you'll get hair down yer back, and all ovah your shirt."

"Had a serious boyfriend once. Thought he was the one. He wasn't. Drank too darn much. Never hit me. That would've ended it."

"Yah know everyone needs someone, but findin someone is hard, and in a small town, you don't have much choice. That's why I came to Atlanta. Needed to get away. Hard to furget though."

TRYING TO BREAK AWAY:

"Yah know, my friend Caitlin and I decided to take a trip to New York. It's always on the news, and seems so glamorous and excitin. All those models dancin at night in clubs. I was unsure about goin -- a little afraid to tell yah the truth. First off, I ain't no model, and I don't get -- or give -- no thrill from wearing a thong with this butt." A quick glance at her hip!

"But, I went along. Whew! What a disaster! Those guys there move fast. That's whole different world. I got to thinkin to myself, yah goin to get in trouble – serious trouble. Bettuh get out!"

"So ladies, you new to New York, uh? Looking for some fun. I can help. I'm your man. Whatta you like? Where you from? Atlanta! Hell, they know how to have a party there." You like to dance? Can you Samba? I can teach you. My name's Horatio! Horatio! What's your name? We're going to have good time tonight. Where you staying? My place is right up the street. Great apartment! Lots of art and stuff – you know Manhattan style."

"After a two nights at some clubs, Caitlin and I agreed, this ain't for us. Jawgiah nevah looked so good. Ain't that somethin! Even when you try to get away, y'ah can't. You are whatcha are! I got Jawgiah genes in me. . . . and I got DKNY jeans at home."

Cassandra smiled, and looked at my face to see if I got her joke. Hunched shoulders, buried neck, raised eyebrows. "That's a good play on words," I said. "I got no comeback for you. I favor Levi's myself."

Cassandra smiled. She knew I was old school. When I told her my age, she said: **Y'ah don't look that old, hon! I'd ah guess, sixty or less. And I a'int sayin that for a tip."** Smile.

GONE WITH THE WIND:

Cassandra went on talking. I suspect she could have cut my hair in five minutes had she wanted. But she wanted to talk -- to share her story. No one was waiting. There was another stylist was sitting in a chair reading a magazine. Cassandra said, **"Don't mind her, she's Russian!** I heard a lifetime in twenty – twenty-five minutes. She knew she could not take too much time, or the camera would get her in trouble.

I gave her a big tip, bought some shampoo, paid in cash, and said, "Thank you! You made me look as good as I can look for an old man. I enjoyed your story." Cassandra smiled. Looked me right in the eyes. **"Thank yah. See y'ah in a few weeks, hon. Y'ah . . . a good man! "**

When I went back four weeks later, Cassandra wasn't there. She had quit or been fired. I asked: "Where's Cassandra – Cass?" "Cassandra doesn't work here anymore." was the quick reply from the girl at the desk.

I asked: "What happened?" The new girl -- an African-American -- replied, "Don't know," nodding her head side to side. Just started working here myself!

"Did she say where she was going to work?" I asked.

"Can't tell you that! I can cut your hair if you want. My name's Tenisha"

BLOWING IN THE WIND:

Cassandra was Georgia. But she was born at the wrong time. I can imagine her singing folk songs in an old bar in the sixties in Greenwich Village: *"How many roads must a man walk down, before they call him a man. The answer my friend, is blowin in the wind . . . the answer is blowin in the wind."*

She would have known why Vladimir was waiting for *Godot,* or she would have asked someone for an explanation – genuine interest in her voice. "So he just waitin, even though he don't know why he's waitin, and he don't mind the waitin." She had a natural inquisitive-ness -- asked questions without offending -- just wanted to know things.

I understood everything too late. I wanted to tell Cassandra she was a good and great person. Behind her soft accent, her warm, natural welcome was a deep, earthy person -- fragile but strong, eager but patient, wanting but waiting; just trying to survive and make it through small-town Georgia.

She was struggling to free herself. She wanted something more, trying to make sense of it all, hoping somewhere along the way there would be an answer to all the contradictions, all the expectations that had not amounted to anything for her.

I can hear Cassandra say to herself: **"Ah did what I was supposed to do. Helped around the house, took care of family, loved my family, even as they kept pullin me down, went to school, staid outta serious trouble. Graduated wantin to know more than I knew, and knowin too late, what I should've done. And then wonderin, 'What the hell happened?**

Where did the time go?' But thah was no one to tell me, no one I could count on to help me along the way. Everyone just seemed to be content to stay the same way, do the same thing everyday. They were satisfied . . . caught?"

In my first visit to the hair salon, I missed seeing the real Cassandra – the combination of sorrow, endurance, quiet rage. Captive to place and time! So much for being a shrink! As I look back on that day, I keep thinking: "I need to see people as more than their roles. Even a quick encounter is a chance to connect, to recognize and to acknowledge someone beyond the fixed role they fill for a job."

Cassandra wasn't a hair stylist, a stranger in a costume, programmed to do a job, to take your money, and then to forget about you the next minute. She was a human being with a life story. She was in need. And so was I. We all are. She knew that. She was sharing. She was reaching out! I missed it! She had no mask. I did! Life's hard on people who don't have a mask.

I don't know what happened to Cassandra. I hope she doesn't take to drinking to make life a little softer on her, or commit suicide a few years from now, giving up. I would like to see her again, and say:

"Thank you. Not for the haircut, but for waking me up! Georgia isn't the same for me now! It's more than red and black and gold and black football colors. Its more than Black revival pastors promising salvation on TV. It's more than fried chicken, barbecue ribs, and "hot-Lanta." It's so much more!

I don't get it all yet, but I am beginning to understand the mystery; why and how Georgia gets under your skin. Why it lingers in memories. Why it holds you. Thanks Cass. I understand why "Georgia is on my mind," in a new way.

POST-SCRIPT:

States, the place, where people are born and raised sometimes take on a special place of identity in their lives, a special meaning that is hard to escape. Georgia is one of the states coming to mind. For many of the people born and raised here in Georgia, there is a special sense of attachment to Georgia, a way of being part of the land, history, and story of the place, there is an identity that becomes part of you, challenging your efforts to be different, inviting you to let Georgia find a place in you, good or bad, giving you a sense of belonging, holding you in grasp, even as you test the roots within you: "No peace, no peace have I."

Paris Past:
The Last Time I Saw . . .

I.

"At least we had Paris!"
> That was the way she ended her note.
>> A bitter sweet ending!
>>> There were good times and bad.
>>>> Paris   kept us together —
>>>>> Paris brought us apart.

We never recovered our past.
> We sensed changes.
>> Time . . . a thousand things,
>>> Had exacted tolls!
>>>> It was not the same.
>>>>> It could never be the same.

We kept reminding ourselves of Paris.
> The kids did not understand.
>> "Why are we eating this stuff?"
>>> Camembert, *coq aux vin*, *pommes frites*, Bordeaux wine,
>>>> All things Paris became a prompt.

Absent place and time,
> We lost what we had,
>> Words were souvenirs.
>>> Yellowed memories!
>>>> It was not enough.

We — well, I — wanted Paris every day,
    Unchanged!
        But without Paris . . .
            And with new lives. . . .

II.

She always knew it was Paris,
    The place, the moments, the freedom!
        I thought it was us,
            She said, "No!
                It was never us."

I remember saying, "Let's go back."
    She smiled, wrinkled her nose.
        "It's too late,
            That's only in the movies.
                We're not Streisand, Redford."

III.

There will always be Paris
    For those wanting love,
        Willing to fall in love completely,
           Willing to trust instincts,
              Willing to let love surround them — like a cocoon.

Willing to be transformed,
    To emerge more beautiful than before,
        To see beauty in the world,
           To understand the beauty they bring.

To be new,
    Attached, connected, joined . . .
        To know each moment,
           The joy of living,
             Living with joy!

IV.

We smiled, we laughed, we cried.
    We were children,
        Delighting in delight!
           Walking in rain,
               Sitting in cafés,
                   Pointing out lovers!

I remember our tears,
    When an elderly couple
        Strolled by . . .
           Beret and scarves — *tres Francais!*
              Holding hands . . . years together.

They nodded to us,
    That all knowing French smile
    That acknowledges love,
        Approves impulse,
           Questions reason!

We were so pleased with our French accent,
    Even when corrected by an *Africaine* waiter:
        "Remember," he said,
           "You must move your mouth when speaking French."

I ordered:
    Le carte pour le dessert, Monsieur.
        Brioche, fromage, vin, une litre, si vous plais.
           "I think I just asked for a cart for the desert?"

It didn't matter.
    Nothing mattered.
        Mistakes were impossible.
          There was only us,
             An eternity of nows!

V.

We — well, I — learned too late:
Passions pass quickly,
Like an unattended garden.
Withering each day,
Without care!

Paris is more than a place,
It is way of being in the world,
Surrounded by indelibles . . .
Buildings, places, faces, beauty, pleasure.
Can there be splendor in air?
Paris stares you in the face
And awaits your surrender!

I spent years trying to understand.
I never felt so alive,
Every cell in my body . . .
Even the world seemed in love.
Problems disappeared,
Vanishing on each street corner.

We found magnificence in ordinary things.
We understood without speaking.
A cup of coffee, croissant, *fromage*, butter,
Was no longer breakfast
It was life.

The walks along avenues, boulevards, side streets.
Rive Gauche!!
Alleys, artists, flowers, postcards.
Notre Dame,
My God!!!
I so wanted it back,
But we never went back.
I wonder if. . . .

VI.

Dear Claire,

> *Thank you for your note,*
> *Especially the last line!*
> *It's my weekend for the kids.*
> *I am humming an old tune:*
> *"The last time I saw Paris. . . ."*

Love, Jack (Jacques) ☺

Comment:

I began writing this poem on August 2, 2012 as the words of a friend echoed in my mind: "At least we had Paris." I finished the poem on August 18, 2012. The words shared were unrelated to what I wrote. But, I must admit, they came at a time when my marriage was under stress, ending in divorce.

I remembered the days I spent in Paris with my wife in the early 1970s. There was something magical about those days. I must admit, we still were young enough to be filled with awe as we walked the streets. I recall our wonder as we tried to figure out the bidet in our hotel room amidst laughter and embarrassment.

My wife and I separated in late 2012, after 49 years and 6 months of marriage. The final divorce decree occurred on March 5, 2014.

Family

I SIT ALONE IN THE NIGHT . . .

I.

1940!
    A weathered, Midwestern-Ohio farmhouse.
        A barren Gothic landscape.
            Rotting wood, rusted-iron fences,
                Unpainted barn and silo.
                    Furrowed ground,
                        Leafless trees.
                            Spring planting complete,
                            Still no signs of life.

In the April dawn,
    A creaking bed.
        Naked bodies sealed,
            Passion, pleasure, pain.
                Oblivious to the fate of their union:
                Unfolding lives.

Bodies sealed in womb walls,
    Amidst a tepid watery world,
        Struggling for space,
            Twisted limbs touching!
                Dominance tested!
                    Temperaments inscribed!

A cold-January dawn,
    A cry pierces gray walls,
        Followed by another,

Cords cut.
Two mouths, only two breasts,
In birth . . . no release.

Life unfolds:
One wins.
One loses.
Forced sharing,
Tears, hugs, smiles,
And silence.

Authoritarian father watches:
Omnipresent!
Pondering the symmetry:
Workers!
Bodies to help!
Girls. . .

Depressed mother, somber, detached,
Aware future sealed,
No escape.
From her bedroom window,
A wire-chicken coop!

A timeless vision of life unfolds.
The chemistry of regret and anger,
Transmitted in fluid and pap!

My wife's mother . . .
Prisoner of unwanted circumstance,
Longing for another life,
Perhaps a teacher, a minister's wife,
A chance to breathe,
To rest at will,
Relief from rules, commands,
Farm rhythms, calendars!

II.

I sit alone now in the night.
    Confronting demons!
        No solace from inchoate shadows from a dim lamp,
           Memories need no light.

Her words echo:
    "It is over!"
        "I am not coming back."
          "I want a new life."

"You can never understand."
    "I want to be with my identical twin.
        It is in my blood!"
        (Known, but unsaid:
        "It was in my mother's blood, her milk!")

Her twin, an omnipresent mirror!
    A life-binding anomaly!
        No escape.

One in conception,
    Then two:
        Miracle, riddle, curse!
          Embedded lives!

III.

Un-blossomed talents,
    Failed opportunities,
        Fulfillment denied.
          Identity unresolved.
            Sullied and withered branches!
              A source needed for blame!

At last love,
>   A city man --
>>   Alive with strength, emotion!
>>>   Marriage,
>>>>   Children,
>>>>>   Harshness escaped.
>>>>>   Flee.

Years pass.
>   Regret.
>>   No escape from her mother's fate.
>>>   Temperament and bonds,
>>>>   Forged in a tortured womb!

Now I sit alone in the night,
>   In a distant time and place,
>>   Victim of an April dawn in 1940,
>>>   A fateful opportunity for passion --
>>>>   A wondrous life-endowing reflex --
>>>>   Now for me a dirge!

Comment:

I wrote this poem on February 9, 2013, 9:30 PM, as I sat alone in the night in a darkened room. My wife of 49 years had left our marriage, seeking to escape from all of marriage's burdens and wounds. I wrote my first lines on a yellow pad as the ironies of my life unfolded before me. I made changes in the poem on March 26, 2013, as my wife returned to resolve financial issues in our separation. I completed the poem on June 2, 2013; time offered me new words and insights.

Parting with Joy . . .

I.

How long did you love me?
  How long did I love you?
    When did it begin?
      When did it end?
        A thousand beginnings and endings!
          On again . . . off again!

Moments, days, years!
  Images blur.
    Feelings erase memories.
      Life now in disarray!
        Can I ever know – understand?

Recall is biased!
  Accuracy requires effort, skill, intent, tactics - -
    Science and art!
      Mnemonics, associations, paths, trails.
        Review . . . renewal!

I never expected departure!
  Never recorded events,
    Daily associations,
      I order chronology,
        Not meaning.

On some days,
  Days celebrating love,

Valentines, anniversaries, birthdays,
Memories return with ease.
A photograph crystallizes time and place.
Context is all!

On others days,
Reminders of your absence
Become painful,
Unbearable!
Clothes left in a closet!
Used make-up in a drawer!
A stream of reminders!

You left behind so much when you
Abandoned me!
Your luggage packed secretly,
While I was ill!
Your plans made across years,
Awaiting the moment!
Courage gleaned from others!

II.

We courted amidst tree-lined college walks,
Ivy-covered walls,
Echoing carillons!
A quarry-stone world,
Secure castle,
Assuming much,
Questioning nothing!

Naive innocence,
Captive to present,
Oblivious to time!
Blinded by love!
Hearts were young,
Confidence strong,

Passions heated,
World awaiting our coming,
With a wry smile!

We walked mortal portals,
Conventional-life corridors,
Sealed by time:
College, schools, house,
Children, family, work!
Details, details,
Life lost in details,
Time for everything,
Time for nothing!

III.

Years passed:
Love, conflict, sorrow,
Annoyance, impatience,
Silent criticisms,
Displayed on face and body!
Apology, healing, repentance!
Endless cycles!

Changes:
Bodies, minds!
Hopes, needs, purposes!
Tolls exacted:
Love, affection, admiration,
Replaced by habit, reflex, routine!
Unexamined assumptions!
Assumed premises!

No efforts after renewal.
Distant vows trusted,
Words forgotten in time,
Distress now in moments, days, months . . .

Limits of disappointment crossed!
Joy gone now . . . in all ways!

Comment:

This is, for me, more than a poem about a failed marriage! It is about love lost! It is an opportunity to recall the joys of courtship and marriage. I began this poem as Joy and I pursued divorce. I did not want a divorce. Joy needed escape! Escape I could understand! But not a permanent loss!

The word "renewal" comes to my mind! Life requires renewal! Marital life does not renew of its own accord. Courtship and marriage require effort, courage, a willingness to test love across time and place, risking much amid changing contexts. And never forget the role of in-laws! March 1, 2013. Recalled June 2, 2015, July 6, 2015 2:24 PM

My Mother's Day

I am old now ...
    But not in my mind's eye.
        From my lifetime eye,
            Millions of memories
                Pass before me,
                    Struggling for attention,
                        Exploration, closure, place.

Faces, events, experiences!
    Winning . . . losing,
        Reminding me who I am,
            Sources of meaning,
                Sculptor of being!
                    Identity . . . identities.

Memories coded as images and emotions,
    Regret, guilt, shame, anger;
        Experiences inscribed,
            Indelibly!
                Incapable of escape!
                    Each moment renewed!
                  Timeless!

I am two!

    My parents quarrel,
        Mother in tears, sobbing,
            Father sulking:

"Shut up!"
Something is wrong!

"We can't go on like this."
"Be quiet, damn it!"
Who said that?
Did I say that?
Who yells?
Who screams?

I am three!

Freshly poured concrete,
Dominates smell!
Darkness!
A basement - damp, cold!
"Why are we here?"
A gray place!
Poles, walls, wires!

Mother lights candles,
Urges me to be silent,
Shussshhhh!
A finger pressed against her lips!
I see her face in flickering light.
An image I will keep for life.
A babuska'd Madonna!
Smiling!
Soothing my fear!

Refuge in basements of unfinished houses,
Awaiting workers to depart,
Entering,
Careful to avoid lumber, nails.
How prophetic!
"Hold on to my hand!"

Mother opens a can of beans,
　　Feeds me with spoon!
　　　　"Did you pay the bill?" she asks.
　　　　　Father turns away!
　　　　　　We are homeless!
　　　　　　　Now I know,
　　　　　　　　But not then!

Blankets spread on a damp, cold-concrete floor.
　　"Go to sleep now, Babe!
　　　Say your prayers."
　　　　I do as I am told!
　　　　　"Now I lay me down to sleep . . . . "
　　　　　Do my words comfort her?
　　　　　　What do they mean?
　　　　　　　"Could I die before I wake?"
　　　　　　　"Could she?"

I am four:

We walk to the bus stop!
　　I hold my mother's hand.
　　　We stop! Await another!
　　　　We step from the bus,
　　　　　Mother holds me,
　　　　　　Smiles,
　　　　　　　Always the smile!
　　　　　　　"It is okay!"

We walk an unfamiliar street,
　　Big buildings!
　　　Traffic!
　　　　No words spoken,
　　　　　It is night,
　　　　　　It is cold,
　　　　　　　I am afraid.

Now I know the story!
But then it was a movie!
Actors playing parts!
Too much to understand!
"Do as you are told!
Do not cause problems!"

We walk south on Euclid Avenue,
Stopping at 86th Street;
Mother looking for an address,
A torn sheet of paper in her hand!
"Regency Hotel!"

We pass a black man begging on the street.
She opens her coin purse,
Gives him some money!
He says: "Thank You!"
She smiles!

"I feel so sorry for them, Babe.
They have nothing."
We pass a White Castle Restaurant.
White tile everywhere,
Bright lights,
Haven from night!
Single shining star!

"I am hungry, Mommy."
We go inside,
Sit on two counter stools.
Mother orders a hamburger and hot chocolate for me.
A cup of coffee for herself!
She wipes my nose with a napkin!
Takes another for herself!

The scene is etched in my mind.
    I remember everything!
        Place, meal, smell, people!
            Years later,
                I search for restaurant and hotel,
                    Spying it from my car window,
                    I stop!
                        Paralyzed by memory!

"Eat, Babe!
    "It is good for you."
        We depart,
            Return to cold night air.
                Mother covers my face,
                    A wool maroon scarf . . .
                        Draped around neck, mouth!
                    Keep out the cold!
                  Protect!

We walk until we reach an apartment building.
    The door is locked.
        An expletive!
            "Oh shit!"
            We wait.

A man comes, enters,
    My mother smiles:
        "We lost our key,"
            How could he turn us away?
            Madonna and child!
            Once again!

We enter,
    Walk up two flights.
        Mother looks at numbers on the door
            Here it is: 204.

She knocks.
She waits.
I watch.
A mystery unfolding!
Sealing my fate!

A door opens,
A man -- my father!
Under shirt and socks!
I know him!
I do not know him!

Mother kneels in tears,
"Joe, please come back."
We need you.
Babe needs you."
Please, Joe!"

"Get the hell out!
Leave me alone!
Get outta here!"

In the background,
I see a woman:
Blonde hair!
In a slip!
I turn away.
Stare at the ground!

The door slams shut!
Mother continues to kneel!
Wiping away tears.
I hear sobs!
I do not look!
I remember!

Mother dies in my arms!
   In a hospital bed,
      I cry! I sob!
         "Mom, I love you so much,
           Thank you, Mom!
             Thank you, Mom.
               Mommmm . . . . . !
                 No! No! No!

Comment:

Mother's Day – May 10, 2015: I am old now . . .

My Stepfather, Stephen

You came into my life when I was eleven years old.
    I stared as you walked down the ship's long gang plank,
        A single cardboard suitcase in hand,
            Leaving behind the Italian liner, *Vulcania*,
                Your home for a bewildering eleven-day journey:
                    Messina, Palermo, Naples, New York City,
                America!
                        Leaving behind the life you had known,
                      For a life unknown!

A swarming crowd of Italian immigrants, visitors, and returning tourists
    Push you forward, all eager to disembark, to greet and be greeted.
        I recall the words of the first passenger on the ground:
            "Oh, it was so bad.
            Storms and high waves all the way.
            I was so sick.
            I am so glad to be here.
            Maria Sanctissima.
            Never again!"

You were gaunt in appearance when I spied you:
    Tall, aquiline nose, high cheek bones, handsome, a sculpted face,
        Proud, almost defiant,
            Looking down from the heights as you descended.
            There was dignity in your slow measured gait.

You had no awareness of what awaited you, Father.
    If you had, you would have returned
        Any possible way,

As soon as possible,
   On the next voyage,
      Had you known!

You searched the crowds for a familiar face.
   I stood next to my mother, Nina.
      She held my hand tightly,
         Yelling, "Steve, Stefano, Stefano! *Caaa!!!!!*"

She let loose her grip,
   Rushing forward to greet you,
      To kiss you, to hug you,
         To look into your eyes, smiling -- alive!
            She would not be denied . . .
               A second chance for love!

She called for me to come.
   You bent and hugged me,
      Staring at me inches away.
         I smelled your cigarette breath.

What did you see in those moments, Father?
   Could you know who I was?
      Could you know where your life would take me?
         Could you know where my life would take you?

I was short, small framed,
   Brown curly hair,
      Prominent bulging dark eyes,
         A preteen awaiting a surge of adolescent hormones
            To fix my features,
               To steady my identity!

My youthful voice — still high-pitched:
   I spoke:
      "*Buon giorno, Padre,*" I said with a Sicilian accent.

> *"Como stai?"*
> *"Io suono priato che lei si qua."*
> *"Io me ciamo, Antonio."*

You smiled, patted my hair,
  Turning now to Nina!
    What did you expect, Father?

Did you expect more from me or Mama?
  Did you expect a savior for your life?
    Someone to buoy your spirits,
      Comfort your fears,
        Salve your wounds,
          Bring you comfort and ease?

We had nothing more to give you, Father,
  Beyond ourselves!
    No money, no position, no hope.
      We looked to you for those things.

Did you understand what you had chosen for your life?
  Did you have even the faintest idea . . .
    The meager fruits and endless burdens
      Thrust upon your rounded shoulders,
        Hunched and bent at 40 years of age
          From years of sculpting and carving
            Marble, granite, rocks, wood!
              Could you know?

There would be no magic in your new life,
  No transforming of stone into gold.
    No alchemy,
      No soothing, bubbling, warm fountains
        To wash away trauma, grief, pain.

We could only give you what we had known:
    Endurance in the face of hardship and disappointment,
       Strength to carry on amid unbearable times,
          Not for moments, not even for days,
             But for years holding on to each other,
               Floating jetsam,
                  Awaiting magical waves to wash ashore,
                 To save us!

Comment:

There is so much I want to say about my step-father, Stephen S. Luparello (1912–1978). He married my mother in 1951 in Italy — a traditional marriage, arranged by family elders: my grandmother, Angelina, and his older brother, Thomas. The words of this poem came to me almost reflexively; I could not type fast enough to get my thoughts on paper. These words are a beginning. I intend to write so much more about this man who gifted my life by sacrificing his in so many ways. Ultimately, his life ended in sadness, not only from malignant cancers destroying his lungs, pancreas, and other organs, but also from a deep sorrow life never offered him the opportunities his talents deserved, and his character warranted.

I am sorry, Father. I did not understand as much as I should have; I did not grasp your total and complete grief at the ill fates life had given you.

Artist in Agony:
My Stepfather, Stephen

I.

He wanted desperately,
    To roar in laughter,
        Hold his sides,
            Gasp for breath,
                Experience glee,
                    Know sheer hilarity!
                        But all manners of pleasure,
                            All moments of happiness,
                          Eluded him!

His mind was sealed by trauma!
    He knew loss!
        He lived pain!
            He witnessed horror!
                He experienced terror!
                He suffered misery!
                    Lifetime imprints!

He wondered:
    How could others abandon control?
        Escape past, feel joy?
            He looked at them – bewildered.
        How? Why?

No answers beyond "destiny" came!
    He recalled Verdi's opera:

La forza del destino!
Aria: *Morir! Tremenda cosa!*
     ("To die, a momentous thing!")
He knew death, seen it, felt it!

II.

Exuberance . . . impossible!
     He was confined to smiles,
          An occasional toss of the head,
               "Sniffs of the nose,"
                    No intentional mirth.
                         Somberness!
                              Laughter with cynicism!
                                   "What do you know?
                                        Do you know what I have seen?"

Momentary pleasures!
     Passed with completed tasks:
          Painting with oils,
               Carving wood,
                    Sculpting clay!
                         Crafting a delicate rosewood mandolin!
                              An artist absent agony!
                                   Passing quickly!

Amusement!
     Sinful!
          Disrespectful!
               Insulting!
                    Demeaning!
                         Do they not know?
                              Have they not seen?

He forced a grin,
     For sake of others,
          Nodding!

Unspoken acknowledgement!
Others tried to please him!
A good meal!
A good cigarette!
    "What do you need Stefano?"

Dark humor was worse!
  A meeting place for pain and pleasure!
    No **Schadenfreud** for him,
      No satisfaction from someone's pain.
      Who benefits from suffering?

Empathy, sympathy, sorrow!
  These he knew well,
    He lived amidst them!
      Images returning with ease.
        Overwhelming him!
          No satisfaction in revenge for him.
        No consolation!

He tried to survive;
  Sought refuge in a new land!
    It was impossible!
      Lived experiences sealed his fate,
        No changes with time or place.
        Torment omnipresent!
          Inscribed, carved, painted,
          In body and mind!

His life caught in time:
  Fixed in an artist's fragile imagination,
    Sensations crying for release,
      Redemption from sorrow's grip!
        War, poverty, hunger,
          Starvation, poverty, death,
          Demons!

III.

He walked:

From Torino to Messina -- 1943:
1381 kilometers by air!
2000 kilometers on swollen feet!
Avoiding roads,
German troops!

He walked:

War over for Italian soldiers,
Partisans fighting!
Germans contemptuous!
Firing squads!
Sites before him engraved!
Reality intaglios!

He walked:

Rome spared,
Even Nazi Generals understood:
"Do not destroy eternity."
Destroy only human lives!
They are expendable
For grand designs!

He walked:

Before him destruction, deprivation,
Disgrace, dishonor!
Open-mouth corpses,
Sagging buildings,
Dust in every breath,
Children begging,
Women – young and old –
Offering emaciated bodies.
Lira! Lira!

He walked:
>With each step,
>>Memories!
>>>Soldier!
>>>>King Victor Emmanuel's Italian Army!
>>>>Spain, Libya, Italy!

He walked:
>*Sopportare!*
>>Bear the unbearable!
>>Smirk!
>>>Hell is life!
>>>Life is hell!
>>>>Fire and brimstone!
>>>>No escape!
>>>>No sanctuary!

He walked:
>Is this what Dante knew?
>>Where is Beatrice?
>>How prophetic: *"Inferno!"*
>>>Poetic words from Petrarch,
>>>>Paintings from Leonardo!
>>>>>Sculptures from Michelangelo!
>>>>>Carvings from Cellini!

He Walked:
>Preoccupations!
>>What matters beauty?
>>What matters heritage?
>>What matters time,
>>>If all can be erased in moments:
>>>>Chest-thumping dictator in balconies,
>>>>>*"Better one day as a lion,*
>>>>>*Than a lifetime as a lamb!"*
>>>>Metaphors!
>>>>Meaningless!

IV.

He welcomed death!
    Not for a glorious cause!
        To flee life!
           His thoughts went beyond impulse:
                He considered place, meaning, time:
                Somber detachment essential!

He went to confession.
    Begged for forgiveness,
        From God,
           From priests,
                From self!
                Why was he begging?

Priests!
    Agents of god . . .
        Why does god need agents?
        Whose side are priests on?

Priests share confessions with bishops,
    Bishops share with the Vatican,
        Vatican stores secret files for posterity!
           Know the truth!
           Hide the truth!
              Vows cast aside!
              Betrayal!

V.

Spanish Civil War:
    Two years, 8 months, 1 day:
        A lifetime of scars!
           Barcelona, Madrid, Guernica:
           An enduring legacy!

Prelude to WWII!
　　Cold-War harbinger!
　　　　Middle-East omen!
　　　　　　Ideologies, prophecies, grand designs!

Global military-industrial-banker complexes,
　　Feasting on death and destruction!
　　　　New nations, faces, places,
　　　　　　Old wine in new bottles!

Factions:

Republicans! Popular Front!
　　Stalinists! Communists! Unionists! Socialists!
　　　　Latvian, Polish, Czech, Garibaldi, Soviet brigades!
　　　　　　Most volunteers, Jewish idealists!
　　　　　　　　An American Brigade!
　　　　　　　　　　Hemingway!
　　　　　　　　　　　　Did he grasp the bell tolls?

Nationalists! Monarchists! Dictators!
　　Franco! Carlists! Fascists! Falangists!
　　　　Catholicism at stake . . . in new ways!
　　　　　　Opus Dei! A rebirth!
　　　　　　　　Godless communists!
　　　　　　　　　　Jews seeking revenge!

Germans! Italians! Spanish armies!
　　Ideologies!
　　　　Nations!
　　　　　　Why?

Modern War:

Statistics!
　　Dead, wounded, MIA,
　　　　Symbols, songs, words:

INTERNATIONALE:

> *Stand up! All victims of oppression,*
> *For the tyrants fear your might,*
> *Don't cling to your possessions.*
> *For you have nothing,*
> *If you have no rights!*

Horst Wessell!
Deutchsland, Deutschland, Uber Alles!
Sieg Heil! Bloodlines protected!

GIOVINEZZA!

> **Hail, People of heroes!**
> **Hail, Immortal Fatherland,**
> **Your sons were born again**
> **With faith and ideals!**
> **Warrior values!**
> **Youth, youth!**
> **In the hardship of life!**

Realities. . .

Idealism in an age of want!
   Nobility in failure!
      Romanticized war posters!
         Dying for country!
            Blood sacrifices offered.

Orders!
   Vodka, wine,
      Charge the hill!
         Futility!
            Potatoes, cabbage, rats!
               Minds, bodies, souls, driven by madness!

Causes forgotten!
Amid stupor!
Primitive survival!

Bandiera Roso!
Red! Blood red!
Round Eastern-European faces,
Stop Fascism,
Stalin's scourge!

Spread the new gospel of the age . . . Communism!
How glorious to die for a cause!
Do not hesitate!
Our cause is just!
(USA supported Franco silently:
"Better dead than Red!" It would never end)

Bodies: Headless, limbless, blood-soaked!
Priests, nuns, altar boys . . . shot!
Churches filled with people praying!
Youth, women, old men!
Burned alive!
Statues shattered!

Republican brigades in red bandanas!
Men . . . women!
Standing nearby:
Staring, spitting,
Contempt-filled faces,
No tears!
Loyalists taking notes!

And then, Loyalists:
You want freedom!
You want equality!
We give you equality,
But for a price!

Stukas! Tanks! *Blitzkrieg*!
    Cold, mechanical, precision metal!
      Ideology no match!
        Lives inconsequential!

The artist in agony:

Confess!
    Reality no longer clear!
      Confess for imagined sins,
        Confess for sins of others!
          Confess for being alive!
            No longer able to remember!
              "Father, Forgive them . . . !"
                Forgiveness . . . for what?

Confess . . . What?

For failing to shoot prisoners!
    For refusing orders!
      For witnessing firing squads!
        For offering water to a dying women,
          Blood-saturated blouse,
            Blue eyes, blonde hair,
              Conscripted for cause!
              "Gracias, Senor!"
                Dying in your arms!

Confess . . . What?

Madness on all sides
    Massacred nuns, priests in black,
      Fascist soldiers in brown and grey!
        Jewish zealots avenging history,
          Still fighting Rome!
            Religious fanatics,
              Protecting God, Mary, saints!

Confess . . . What?

For living!
For turning from torture,
For wanting to breathe air free of dust and blood,
For chewing stale bread,
When bread no longer mattered;
For quenching thirst
With mud-slaked water!

Confess . . . What?

Once my Stepfather told me:
"Hunger does not know bad bread!
Fame no conosce pani malo.
Manga!"

Finish your food!
Mama worked hard to cook it.
I worked hard to place it on the table.
I nodded in agreement.
He was right!"
How could I know sources of his words?

IV.

His mind began crumbling,
Years before,
In the absence of hope!
Can tapestry be weaved
From broken strands, fibers . . . burned embers?

In his life:

His mother lost to war,
His sister to disease,
His father to work!

His brother prisoner-of-war:
Insults and humiliation,
Barbed-wire fences,
English guards pointing rifles
Eager to shoot,
Daring prisoners to run
For practice!

Post-War Italy:

Chaos! Confusion! Deceit! Betrayal!
Communists, Fascists, Socialists, Anarchy!
Fifty governments in ten years!

And from America, . . . Operation Gladio!
American CIA and Italian governments conspired.
Communism must be stopped in Italy,
At any costs!
Blood in the streets!
Assassinations, beatings, conspiracy!
Choose sides!
Choose corruption!
Choose cronyism!
Choose evil!

Escape to America!
He wrote to his brother.
His new land was not what he expected.
No respite offered!
Poverty!
No opportunity!
America: Illusion!

His hopes failing!
Every word an offense!
Every day a burden!
His wife and son . . . kind and caring;

He needed more!
Escape from past,
Freedom from present!
Renewal!
Return to place!
Habits, reflex, routine!

V.

I once saw him laugh . . . uninhibited,
Unrestrained!
Almost hysterical!
Vino et veritas!
I welcomed his joy!
It never returned!

He was slightly drunk:
Too much wine!
In our house,
A dinner, a small gathering,
My European friends!

He told a story of a night in Barcelona,
As a soldier in King Emanuel's army,
Amid the horror of civil war!
He was drunk – Spanish wine!
He was unable to walk!

To demonstrate,
He rose from his chair,
Got on hands and knees!
Mimicked crawling back to camp!
Saluting gate guards from a prone position!
He laughed hilariously!
All reserve gone.
How wonderful to see laughter!

My guests laughed less!
　　They were from Eastern Europe,
　　　　Family members served
　　　　　　In Stalin's Communist Brigades in Spain!
　　　　　　Relatives lived in Post-war Italy.

No word was spoken!
　　Their glances sufficient!
　　　　He did not notice!
　　　　　　I did!
　　　　　　　　Endless vengeance!

What does one do?
　　When suffering is daily fare?
　　　　Trauma sealed in mind, muscle, bone,
　　　　　　Images, sounds, smells!
　　　　　　　　Puncturing the soul!
　　　　　　　　　　No respite! Again and again!
　　　　　　　　　　Freud knew: **Repetition-compulsion!**

Distance, detachment, somberness!
　　Energy suppressed,
　　　　Frivolity foolish!
　　　　　　Happiness eluded,
　　　　　　　　Life questioned!
　　　　　　　　　　No escape!
　　　　　　　　　　An artist in agony!

Lyrical Poems: The Blues

**Sung in a Plaintive Voice and Mood –
Sullen and Helpless – Resigned – With a Hint of Survival**

- *Useless Man Blues*
- *Irish Lady Blues*
- *I Am so Tired of Pickin Cotton*
- *Jane…Plain and Simple*
- *Saturday-Night Woman…*
- *Breaking Free Blues*
- *The Way of the Blues…*

Useless Man Blues

I.

There's nothing more to say, Mama,
I heard all before,
There's nothing more to say, Mama,
Stop pointin at the door!

I just need to sit here quiet, Mama
Thinkin my sorrow through.
I am tired and weary,
Got the useless man blues . . .

II.

Don't make me feel useless,
That's an easy thing to do,
Don't make me useless,
I've got holes in my old shoes.

I need some lovin Mama,
We been through this before,
Stop shoutin at me, baby,
Stop pointing at the door!

III.

I just need to feel wanted,
Held tight in my baby's arms,
I just need to feel wanted,
Honey, turn on some lovin charm.

Can you understand me, Mama?
Keep your cat-tongue tied,
Can you understand me Mama?
My insides have already died.

IV.

There's nothing more to say now,
I heard it all before,
There's nothin more to say now,
Stop pointing at the door.

I understand your feelins, Mama.
Bout paying all the bills;
I understand your feelins, Mama
I know you need your pills.

V.

But there's nothin I can do now,
Just drink your Ripple wine,
Everything you say now, woman
Is killin me inside.

There's nothing left for hurtin,
Everything's gone and died.
Not arguing with you, Mama,
Just listen to my side.

VI.

I agree with what you're saying!
I know I am no good too!
It's hard for me to say it,
I got the useless man blues.

Useless man blues ...
I got the useless man blues.

Irish Lady Blues

I.

Well I know an Irish Lady,
   She lives just south of town,
      She runs a jumping bar there,
      People come from miles around.

Oh Irish Lady,
   You are Mama to us all,
      Irish Ladyyyyy . . .
         300 pounds . . . and six feet tall.

Tell me Irish Lady,
   How did you get this way?
      Fillinggg shot glasses,
      For IOU's and no pay!

Irish Lady,
   You are Mama to us all,
      Oh Irish Ladyyyy,
         Pickin us up when we fall.

II.

Now what's special bout this Lady,
   When she's done tendin bar,
      She puts on her rhinestones,
         And gets set to be the star!

She struts to spotlight,
    Set to break the rules.

        She stares straight ahead,
            And she starts singin the blues.

Oh Irish Lady,
    You are Mama to us all
Irish Lady,
    You lift us up when we fall.

Now you got to see this Lady,
    People come from Orleans' town,
        Platinum hair and green eyes,
            But her skin is chocolate brownnnnn.

Oh Irish Lady,
    You are Mama to us all,
Irish ladyyyy,
    Liftin our spirits when we fall.

Imagin this beauty before you,
    Platinum hair, chocolate skin,
        Cat-eyes all aglowin,
            Unafraid of singin sin!

Ohhhh, Irish Lady,
    Let me hear those mournful sounds,
        No one else can do it like you,
            You lift us up when we are down.

Oh Irish Lady,
    You is, who you is,
        You just sing your heart out, Mama,
            Its religion, its not biz.

Ohhh, Irish Lady,
    Tell me your secret to survive,
        We know you got no money,
          Yet you always seem to thrive.

III.

Soooo, here is her story,
    You been waiting to be told,
        It's a well-known story,
          People once were bought and sold.

But some good people stood up,
    Said that's not for me.
        Bought papers, broke shackles,
          They set Black folks free.

IV.

Way down in the bayou,
    There was a man named "O'Toole."
        He was a giant of a man, eyes crystal blue.

Everybody loved him.
    He was kind, wasn't cruel,
        Unlike others around him,
          He lived the golden rule.

One day he was out walkin,
    Searchin for his life.
        He spied a chocolate lady,
          Asked her to be his wife.

They moved from the Bayou,
    Started a bar right on this spot,
        Comfort food, beer, and chicken,
          It was good cold or hot.

Oh Irish Ladyyyy,
    You are Mama to us all.
        Singing blues while you pout,
            You are the story . . . of the South.

I AM SO TIRED OF PICKIN COTTON

An African American Blues Anthem

I.

I am so tired of pickin cotton,
Pickin cotton in my dreams!
I can still hear the whiplashes,
I can still hear the screams.

I am tired of pickin cotton,
Risin up from the floor!

I want rest from slavin,
Still happenin at this time,
Lord give me a reason,
I ain't standin in moh lines!

Let me walk without hunchin,
I want freedom today.
I ain't pickin cotton,
No moh, anyway!

II.

Five centuries ago,
They brought us to this land,
Shackled and bound up,
Neck, feet, ankles, and hand.

No watuh when we was thirsty,
No food to feed the young,

Scars across our bodies,
Threatin to cut off our tongues.

I ain't pickin cotton.
Never again no more,
No more cotton pickin.
I ain't bendin,
Not even to the Lawd.

No mercy shown to us,
We had no place to turn,
We were sold just like cattle,
Let me die, that's what I yearned.

What did we do, Lawd,
We didn't do no sins,
Oh Lawd, it was you Lawd,
Gave us the color of our skins.

I ain't pickin cotton,
For no one anymore,
You bettah hear my words now,
I ain't telling you no more.

III.

When we wailed, and tried to stand.
The man said we would be sold,
Just listen to your mastuh,
Do as you're told!

Forced by greed and wicked people,
Demons one and all,
Using guns, whips, and chains,
As man-made law!

No moh cotton,
Not even in mah clothes,
Cotton turned people,
Into every man's foe!

He yelled at us to be quiet,
Don't sing no moh songs,
He told us he was our ownah,
He was our god now, and long.

You are black heathens,
Nothin moh, nothing less.
Bodies for pickin cotton,
Day and night with no rest!

No rights and no justice,
Continues to this day,
I ain't gonna take this,
No moh, anyway!

I claim my manhood,
Claim it right now!
You can shoot me and beat me,
I refuse to be cowed!

I am standin, not weepin!
Lookin you in the face,
You can't do no moh to me,
I will no longer runaway!

My feet are firmly planted,
My body is erect,
I ain't pickin no moh cotton,
In dreams, or in the flesh!

You'd bettah start thinkin people,
Bout your treasured golden rule,
Cause you are lookin at a Black man,
He ain't no longah gonna be a fool.

If not it's all ovah,
All ovah for us all . . .
We either live together,
Or we are allllll, gonna fall.

Jane . . . Plain and Simple
A Ballad of a Mining-Town Woman

I.

They call me Jane . . . plain and simple;
That's the name they give to me,
They call me, Jane . . . plain and simple,
That's just what they see.

But they only know the outside,
They don't know the heart inside of me!

Here is my story,
Judge me on your own,
See if what their sayin,
Deserves their mockin tones.

I live in a trailer park,
Just South of town,
Three kids below eight,
And a wheelchair-bound, Mom.

They call me Jane . . . plain and simple;
That's the name they give to me,
But they only know the outside,
They don't know the heart inside of me!

II.

I take any work I'm offered,
Moppin floors, cleanin seats,

Grateful for the money,
Sleepin with no pillows and no sheets.

One day life my life was shattered,
Its' never been the same,
I learned people can be evil,
Some people escape feelin shame.

III.

There were times we were livin,
Up high on the hog.
Had food, clothes, and housin,
Beer, dancin, and folk songs;

Can't say we were in heaven,
But no one was really down.

But nothin lasts forevuh,
That's the truth I have found.
One day your feelin up,
And the next day you are down.

IV.

On a day just like others,
Our life was to change,
The dirty mine owner,
Took our money, and ran away.

Some men said he can't do this,
Went home, and got their guns.
Caught the mine owner,
Shot him dead on the run.

They knew what they were doin,
There were people all around.

Our men just stood there ovah him,
With no smile or no frown.

V.

Everyone said it was justice,
But the law said it was not!
The men were tried and sentenced,
And the mine was nailed shut.

No use now in crying,
No one helps those in need,
The rich just look down upon us,
And say: "Sell me your deed."

VI.

One day, if I'm lucky,
Gonna leave this place,
Get on a bus with mah kids,
Leave town without a trace.

Put memories behind me,
Let people forget my face.

VII.

For the moment, I am existin,
It's a matter of cash,
I'm livin as I am dyin,
The rich call us white trash.

I just ignore their harsh words,
They ain't sittin on no thrones.
They wouldn't last a minute,
Living my life . . . weary to the bones.

They nevah get to thinking,
There are heart and minds
In what they see,
They only see the outside,
They don't know the hurt in me.

VIII.

There is some hope in me though,
I found my old guitar,
Been playin in the moonlight,
And prayin to the Lawd.

I know the lawd is with me,
Hears me cryin in my plight.
Listens to my singin,
Gives me strength day and night.

They call me Jane, plain and simple,
That's the name they give to me,
They call me Jane, plain and simple,
They don't see the hope . . . inside of me . . .

Saturday-Night Woman . . .

I.

Just waiting for the right man,
To come into my life,
Bring me wine and roses,
Be with me day and night!

It's always what I think of,
When working, or at play.
Waiting for the right man,
To come to me, and to stay!

I keep humming all those love songs,
With words making me believe,
There's magic in the moonlight,
And love is what I need.

But maybe that's all deception,
It is not what it's made up to be,
It's possible they been making money,
Appealing to my fantasy!

Been waiting for a long time,
Maybe its time for me to choose,
Stop waitin for the right man,
And end my daily blues.

II.

Don't need no Saturday-night lover,
Torrid and sensual as he can be,
Leaving me gasping for breath,
Shouting, "Oh my God, Oh my God,
. . . Save me!"

I enjoy that special moment,
When I'm released like a tide,
Muscle and bone's quivering,
Keepin my lover deep inside!

III.

But nothing lasts forever,
Your love can't be a ride,
You need to treat love special,
It must stay, and it must abide.

Just because you feeling good now,
Doesn't mean all is well,
There's life outside a bedroom,
And for many, that life is hell.

I am more than just a body,
I must remember that all the time,
I must not surrender to the moment,
Even if it is sublime!

IV.

I am a woman,
I'm tired of believing lies,
Gonna start a new day,
I'm done with night-time tries.

I am now seeing,
Clearer than before,
A woman must first find herself,
That's the secret . . .
That's the open door!

That's the secret . . . The open door.
Done waiting for the right man,
No longer . . . any more.

Breaking Free Blues

I.

Baby, Baby, Baby . . . you are no good for me!
Baby, Baby, Baby . . . we are now history!

I kept hoping I could change you.
Make you a man who loves me!

But I can see that ain't likely,
Given what you are!
You got a demon deep inside you,
In place of a heart!

You live for the moment,
For white powder and pills,

Inhale weed wrapped in paper,
Just waiting for the thrill!

II.

You ain't going nowhere,
It took me so long to see,
You are sliding downward,
And you were dragging me.

I ain't going with you,
You are all **alone** now,

You can follow your demon,
Right up to the gates of Hell.

Baby, Baby, Baby . . .
You're a man in disguise.
Speaking pretty words when needed,
Trying to hypnotize!

But I see through the smoke now,
Cost me five years of my life,
I am leaving you, Baby,
Breaking free from trouble and strife!

III.

I hate the times when you grab me,
With powder-filled hands.
Throw me on the bed,
Make me yield to your demands.

Let me call your attention,
Just remember last night.
I put on silk and satins,
Closed down all the lights,

Lit some scented candles,
Tried to make the evening just right.

But you said: "I am going out now!"
Threw pills on the bed,
Told me to try some,
Said they're called "Devil's Head."

IV.

So pack your bag, get moving!
Want none of your stuff.
No more lies and rejection,
I am calling your bluff.

Stop looking at me like that!
Tearful eyes don't work no more!
Begging and pleading for forgiveness,
Feet shuffling, eyes staring at the floor,

I am done with you, Baby.
Do you hear what I say?
You can leave anytime,
Just get out of my way!

I am free now!
Going to make a new life,
Spoke to the lawyer, Baby,
I am no longer your wife.

The Way of the Blues . . .

I.

"And old man approached me . . .
As I was standing on the street:"

**"Pretty woman. . . you look tired!
Pretty woman . . . you look beat!"**

"At first I was suspicious!
What did this man intend?
Had too many men before him,
Try to lead me into sin!"

II.

He said: **"Look here pretty women,
I know what's on your mind,
I ain't hitting on you, Mama,
Need no dollar or a dime."**

The old man then asked me:
"Do yah know how to singggg the blues?"

I replied: "I'm just survivin,
I always seem to lose!"

Then he said to me gently:
**"Hear my words, what I say,
When you try, and you lose,
That's the time to sing the blues."**

III.

"See, you sing the blues,
When you're angry!
You sing the blues,
When you're sad,
Sometimes yah even sing
The Blues when you're glad."

"See singing blues is like praying,
When times are really bad!"

"Blues bring you comfort,
In rhythm and rhyme,
Try singing with me, Honey!
I got nothing but time."

IV.

Then he reached over,
Opened a weathered-leather case,

Pulled out an injured guitar,
Put a smile on his face.

He said: "Look here pretty women!
You're the one, I've been looking for."
I wander up an down these roads,
Trying to find someone hurtin to the core!

"Listen to me, Mama!"
"I know you can sing with grace,
It's in the way you're standing,
It's in the lines on your face."

V.

"So I started humming,
At first mournful sounds,
Then I started praying,
And the words were just found."

"My body started moving,
Not of my accord,
It just seemed to happen,
Felt my sorrows with each chord."

"My eyes started tearing,
I had no control,
The words and music just were coming,
From deep inside,
My soiled soul!"

"I felt a newborn feeling,
I was no longer alone.
I was part of something bigger,
I knew I had found a home."

"I understood in that moment,
What "amazing grace" really means.
How the blues can connect you,
To a new-way-of- being!"

Thank you, thank you, Old Man,
Wherever you may now be,
Walking dusty streets and highways,
Setting lives free!

War

Walt Whitman Returns . . .

"This is what you shall do:
Love the earth and sun and the animals,
Despise riches,
Give alms to everyone that asks . . .

I.

Again! Again!
Hate's fiery cauldron overflows!
No lessons learned!

Battlefield tolls unheeded:
Gettysburg, Manassas, Chancellorsville, Vicksburg?
More than places!
Sacred lands, defiled!

Unshaven old men,
Pimpled-scarred youth,
Blue or grey, now red!
Bodies lying in heaps . . . or alone,
Limbless, moaning, seared souls,
Dead!

Posterity captured:
Rifles in hand, pistols gripped, swords unsheathed,
Bloodstained rocks, smoldering earth, shattered trees.
Flies gathering to feast,
Buzzing amid charnel,
Choosing choice sites!

II.

Brave soldiers march to cadenced drums.
Flags wave,
Artillery towed,
Medaled-generals salute,
Parades!
"Charades" . . . I say!

Battles forgotten,
Triumph's costs denied.
Music and verse:

> *"Mine eyes have seen the glory . . ."*
> *"Oh, I wish I was in the land of cotton …*
> *"Onward Christian soldiers . . ."*

And in the background,
Still in shadows,
Time unchanged:

> *"Steal away, steal away; Steal away to . . .*
> *"Deeeppp river, Lawd! My home is over Jordan.*

"Illusions . . . delusions," I say!
Podium, stage, pulpit,
Platforms for death and destruction;
Foundations for domination!

How inadequate Periclean words,
Unfit for all times.
Preserving lies!
Inspiring myths!
Nurturing cultures of war,
Cults of nations,
Food for empire!

144

III.

Did you not see what I saw?
Endless rows of blood-stained sheets,
Gaunt nurses placating life,
Tears streaming from bedside widows,
Hollow-eyed children,
Begging for bread.

Charred houses,
Broken bridges,
Shattered trees,
Smoldering carcasses,
Stench like no other!

Damn the cannon makers!
Damn the smelters making them!
Damn the voices cheering their firing!
Guiltless!
Blind to their sullied metal fruit,
Deaf to cries,
Distance from shot to crater,
Buffering conscience!

I say:
Make them walk brimstone,
Breathe fumes of seared flesh,
Beg for mercy,
Ask respite from hot metal,
Seek relief from scorched earth.

Make them know pain, suffering, death -
Avoided – escaped – denied
Hidden amidst comforts of
Gilded rooms,
Leather chairs,
Polished tables,

Sycophants:
> "Sir!"
> "No, Sir!"
> "Yes, Sir!"
> "More, Sir?"
> Sherry, Sir?

IV.

What use conscience?
What value brain?
What function heart?
What glory courage . . .
If ignored, denied, separated
From a silent human face.

A face, once admired and prized,
Bursting forth from a mother urging
Her swollen womb;
Grunting . . . screaming
Unfathomable mysteries,
Birthing life!
A face emerges!
Its future inscribed.

Tear down your crosses, crescents, and angled stars.
You ignore their precepts.
Excuses for madness,
Salve for betrayal,
Gloves for stained hands,
Veils for truth!

Fall upon your knees,
Beg forgiveness,
Judas!
Failed prophets!
Flawed angels!

God pretenders!
Soiler of time and place!

Mortal art thou, Man!
Blood, bone, sinew.
Seeker!
Mind!
Spirit essence!
Sing the song of life:
Cast seeds upon the land,
Plant trees in barren hills,
Water fallow fields!

Look to mountains,
Forested woods,
Desert sands,
Mirrored lakes,
Gaze in wonder!

Inhale air,
Sip water,
Break bread,
Behold skies;
All else is vanity!

Go now:
Walk tortoise paths,
Follow hare tracks,
Eat berries,
Urinate,
Create streams - droplets!
Erase scars of war!

All is sacred!
Behold grandeur,
Fill senses with awe –

Failing this,
Know you never lived!

At end of day,
Earth will accept your
Crumbled remains,
And . . . try again!
And you will have no choice!

V.

"This is what you shall do:
Stand up for the stupid and crazy,
Devote your income and labor to others,
Hate tyrants, argue not concerning god,
Have patience and indulgence toward the people,

Re-examine all you have been told
At school or church or in any book,
Dismiss whatever insults your own soul;
And your very flesh shall be a great poem."

> *Walt Whitman*
> *Preface to Leaves of Grass*
> *(1855)*

Comment:

Walt Whitman (1819-1892) is my favorite poet – and in many ways, my favorite humanist. He witnessed the horrors of the American Civil War -- its sights, sounds, and smells inspired his commitment to peace. But long before the War, his special senses gave voice and word to the changing world about him. He captured time and times! He was subject to human frailties as we all are; yet his contributions endure because of their obvious commitment to peace and justice.

I find life in his every word -- each line and verse, a sacred-clarion call to life! In his words - their pace, stridency, boldness - spring passionate observations, accusations, and visions of hope revealing uncommon and uncompromising courage and wisdom.

I wonder what Walt Whitman would say if he appeared in our time? I know he would recognize the betrayal of history's lessons – humanity's continued infatuation with violence and war. He would scold us! Reprimand us! Remind us solutions are to be found in compassion and connection -- not metal.

I tried to channel him: I wrote a draft of this poem in hours the next morning and early day. I waited a few days, overwhelmed by my efforts to hear his voice, to channel his presence. It is best to rest when you awaken the dead. My words lack the power and grace of Walt Whitman; but I am consoled by the fact, my intention is his!

12/13/2014 at 9:49 AM -- On this day, about this time, decades ago, my step-father, Stephen, as good a man as ever walked the earth, died in my arms. Among his final words: ". . . How tragic so few have chances to develop their talents . . . ."

"Two Paths in the Wood:"
"Choice" of Life or War

The Road not Taken . . .

Two roads diverged in a yellow wood,
And sorry I could not travel both. . . .

Somewhere ages and ages hence,
Two roads diverged in a wood,

And I . . . And I took the one less traveled by.
And that has made all the difference.

Robert Frost
Pulitizer Prize American Poet
(1874-1963)

"Choice:" Poetic, Personal, and Political

Literary critics have written much of this popular Robert Frost poem. All seem to agree that the essence of Frost's poem is the importance of "choice" in the absence of any knowledge of possible consequences" -- the making of an important decision without knowing the likelihood of the outcomes. This decision requires the willingness to make a "choice" based on personal confidence, trust, and, perhaps more than anything else, courage.

Critics suggest Frost understood in his poem there was no better path, but rather "choice" is our daily reality – "choice" is present in each and every moment, and "choice" is inherent in the nature of human life, and forms the basis for individual and social morality.

Unlike other species relying on reflexive, inborn fixed-response patterns, humans have the capacity for "choice," albeit, in many, there is little conscious awareness of this special capacity. As life unfolds, the consequences of our "choices" reveal the wisdom (i.e., fulfillment, satisfaction, comfort), and/or regrets (i.e., remorse, penitence, guilt, trauma) of our life.

I chose Frost's poem as a departure point for a "choice" all humans face at this time in our world. In my opinion, the "choice" is between endless war – endless killing and destruction -- or the nurturing and sustaining of life. Here I could substitute the word "peace," but I am uncertain at this point what peace means. People, societies, and nations use the word peace with impunity to benefit their own needs, rather than a source of mutuality -- an enduring state and condition in which violence, destruction, and war are refused. Enough!

I am asking for a world free of strife, suffering, agony, and endless pain and grief. The mythical apocalyptic horses are exacting their legendary tolls, poverty, famine, disease, and war, amidst threats of extinction, disposal lives, and exhaustion of natural resources. We are living in the *Anthropocene Era* (epoch, age) in which human behavior – shaped by "choice," is the dominating force shaping our world's survival. The two greatest capacities of humanity -- consciousness and conscience – have yielded to denial and avoidance in favor of reflex and impulse. *Cui Bono?*

Beyond Symbolic and Poetic Words

The path we choose in our lives is *not* merely a symbolic or poetic path -- one presented so eloquently by Robert Frost's image of worn and less-trodden paths at a fork in the road. **No!** The path before us is an essential life nurturing and sustaining path -- each person must choose to renounce violence, destruction, war, and killing. In each of daily habitual actions, we are making moral choices regarding the survival of our planet.

Humanity is at the point of extinguishing countless life forms and expressions. We engaged in an unbridled assault upon each other and upon the natural world. Our appetites for destruction are endless in virtually every realm of our lives -- economic, political, social, educational, and moral. Our global condition is well–known, and yet we are oblivious to the dangerous consequences we are supporting.

These facts are most visible in the United States of America, a nation one symbolized as a "beaming light-on-the-hill," and now an example of a nation most visible whose policies and actions -- whose "choices" -- are characterized by corruption, cronyism, exploitation, violence, inequity, prison population disproportions, and the sins of affluence (i.e., lobbyists, hypocrisy [*hypocracy*], contempt for citizen rights and participation [*demonocracy*], and slow deaths by obesity, malnutrition, racism, classism, poverty).

The mass media, a potential voice for informing and educating citizens is a participant in destruction. Analyses of critical news events become opportunities to defame the "other side" -- what ever that may be! Receptive audiences choose to watch and to listen to media supporting their existing views. And news readers begin to all look similar in appearance and opinion. Minds become closed to doubt. Here I call attention to the more invisible and elusive acts destroying people's lives through assaults on character and personhood via gossip, calumny, half-truths, entrapment, stereotypic names and words, and falsehoods, misrepresentations, and quick-lathered false descriptions.

Enemies of the State . . .

There is a popular tactic used by "national security agencies" to neutralize critics. The tactic involves not interfering with an individual's efforts to promote peace and social justice, and to be a voice for moral actions. However, simultaneously, agencies are collect and collate extensive information from surveillance, monitoring, and archiving from distant years. At some point, if the critic becomes to "unbearable" to the agency (agencies), they simply begin the process of neutralization by releasing "offensive" information gleaned from many sources, and systematically destroying character and moral standing.

All our lives involve sins of commission and omission. Some are apparent and well-known. Others may be buried in the privacy of the critic's soul. But for agencies intent on "neutralization," they engage in building a systematic profile designed to destroy the words and ideas of the critic. This is done by using different cooperating sources to affirm their conclusion. Was this not what occurred in Nazi Germany, STASI East Germany, Fascist Italy, Communist USSR, North Korea – "Enemies of the State." Is this not what is happening in the USA and its allies?

These destructive acts, whether done by a person, society, or nation, are equally violent and devastating, leaving scars on minds and bodies that are painful and memorable for the agony they have carried. We accuse, vilify, slander, denigrate, abuse, and malign individuals, groups, races, religions, nations, and the very planet on which we live through choices we make and utter each day. This is the way it begins! This is the root of hate and violence. This is the seemingly innocent path that leads so easily to broader acts of violence, destruction, killing, and war.

Consider the reality we are faced with each day as individuals, groups, societies, and nations use the media for propagandistic purposes to justify their actions. We vilify individuals and we vilify nations, it doesn't matter. What we are doing is destroying any possibility of peace. I viewed and a person on TV -- so obviously filled with hate and vengeance toward Muslims -- that he could barely disguise the fire in his eyes, and his advocacy of their destruction.

Here, I am speaking not only of select individuals or groups who have taken it upon themselves under the guise of local, government, or commercial security groups using religion, nationalism, or profit, to kill without remorse (e.g., *Boko Haram*, "secret" black-operation national assassination/drone units, murder- for-hire-groups, or a score of other groups used by governmental, business, or criminal organizations).

Indeed, "terrorism" is precisely what is being used by both small organized "terroristic" groups seeking rebellion and change, and by terrorist nations seeking to impose their will and interests upon others for selfish benefit. There are "terrorist" individuals, nations, businesses, agencies, organizations, societies, and criminal organizations. What do we mean when we say societies and nations have "counter-terrorist" agencies designed to prevent "terrorism," to keep us secure?

At some point, we engage in the very same actions, with the same purposes, and with the same consequences (e.g., see T. Kapitan, October 19, 2014, The Resign of Terror, *NY Times, Opinionator.* See also A.J. Marsella, (2014): **https://transcend.org/tms/2014/10/the-paradoxical-consequences-of-usa-counter-terrorism-programs**).

Beyond Propaganda, Media Deception, and Lies

The United States of America, and its closest international allies, have chosen the path of war, with tragic consequences for the survival of humanity and our natural world. Our foreign and domestic policies are destructive -- serving the political, economic, and financial interests of a limited number of individuals and organizations. Unless we retreat from this path, and choose the path of peace, we will find ourselves doomed to endless domestic and international and violence and war.

The USA has fashioned an explicit global domestic and foreign policy characterized by reliance on encouraging endless fractures and divisions between and among nations, regions, gender, religions, ethnic groups/races, and social-economic classes. We are pitting humanity against itself and against the natural world. We are promoting global chaos and collapse.

Efforts by the USA to use the deceptive "patriotic" attractions and seductions of war -- blindly mantled in glory, soldiers 'bravery, and martial domination, replete with songs, parades, banners, and celebrations of victory and nationalism are deceptive attractions and seductions of our bodies, minds, and spirits. How many more must die from this lie that finds virtue in war? How many more must be wounded, traumatized, and punished by starvation, torture, and social upheaval and dislocation?

Have we no conscience? Have we lost all sense of human dignity and worth? Have we no awareness of our assault on nature? Have we no sense of the exploitation and exhaustion of our natural resources? And still, our leaders come before us, offering their plaintive explanations designed to sculpt their destructive legacy in our minds as legacies of brilliant strategy, moral and ethical choices, and wise and learned tactics and actions. Do they hope that by daily repetition, humanity will believe their lies? Or do they hope by repetition and habituation, they will be released from their duplicity?

Consider this viewpoint: Government is engaged in advertising, propaganda, "strategic communications," with the same purposes as those of a used-car salesperson attempting to sell a malfunctioning and damaged car. The words and intentions are the same:

"Here is our product! Believe me! It is a good product, and you should purchase it! Accept my advice. It would certainly make me happy if you did. (I have used music, color, jingoism, sensuality, and quick and rapid changes of my on-screen message to convince you my product is a good one. And I know you are too uninformed -- too victim to TV – too comfortable to not believe me. I am your demon disguised as your friend)."

The Endless Cycle of War

I do not quarrel with the reality there are nations, groups, and individuals seeking to punish us, and to destroy us. This is accurate!

But I question the absence of understanding reasons for this plight. In my opinion, efforts after violence, war, and terrorism attributed to "envy" are spurious. Those acting against us as a society, culture, and nation perceive us as seeking their destruction. They do this for revenge, and they do this to indicate they will not succumb to defeat. They do this because the USA is now seen across the world as the most dangerous nation – a "bully" willing to impose interests without conscience.

1. "Exceptionalism" and Identity

As a nation, we have lost the trust and respect of many people and nations. Our distorted sense of American "exceptionalism" has led us deeper and deeper into endless wars. This antiquated 19th Century vision and ideology cannot be continued. It is a denial of the reality of our interdependent times in which nations and people seek freedom from external interference. Identity has become a major theme of revolt and rebellion. "I do not wish to have your identity imposed on me – I am aware of the many overt and covert ways you seek to gain control over me." This thought is occurring in many minds across the world. The lessons of empire abuse are not lost!

What do we expect? Can any other response be expected from those we have abused, occupied, killed, and destroyed with an endless array of weapons that defy imagination in their power and cold precision in bringing death? Can any other response be expected from billions of people whose identity, honor, and heritage we have demonized and insulted? Would we permit humiliation of this scope without anger and a willingness to die? How can we expect those seeking our destruction to offer us respect, admiration, cooperation, and peace as we kill their people and destroy their lands?

2. War: Pursuing Grand Designs

The expressed need for a single global power with extensive financial, political, military, and technological expertise has been used to justify the continuation of the USA's domestic and foreign policies and actions. Consider the fact that the USA and NATO have taken actions to surround Russia and China with nuclear warheads and other military weaponry throughout Eastern Europe and Asia. The result is to push Russia and China into defensive postures for self-protection. The cycle is endless, and is reinforced by a score of other actions. Trade pacts that serve to destroy the economies of those who criticize the USA cannot bring peace. When we seek answers to world peace, we must look in the mirror, and consider what we are doing to perpetuate violence, war, and destruction.

The United States of America acts with impunity, disregarding the wishes of others, buying our way into their land and culture with billions of dollars paid to corrupt leaders. We impose our will, interests, and troubled popular culture upon others. Who is making these decisions keeping us in a state of war for more than 200 years, devoid of empathy or compassion for others – committed to the financial and political interests of the purveyors of death?

We have failed in every effort at nation-building because the "transparency" of our efforts is apparent. Military occupation and building huge fortress embassies in Iraq and Afghanistan does not signal purity of intention. They signal our intention to remain in the location, and to control a nation's destiny for our selfish interests. This cannot lead to peace.

The USA's wars on poverty, terrorism, crime, and drugs are massive failures reflecting an ignorance of the complex social, economic, political, and cultural realities of our times. Has a powerful shadow government developed in the USA that transcends our troubled executive, congressional, and judicial branches? Have national and domestic security become justifications for increasing control and domination via surveillance, monitoring, and archiving of all our legal rights and privileges? A recent USA government report indicates our policies lack justification and effectiveness. They are subject to major flaws in our judicial process, tainting it with favoritism, accommodations to special interests, and an absence of reform.

The Path of Empire Building and Collapse

Unlike the uncertainty of Frost's paths, our "choice" as citizens of the world is clear. We can no longer continue, for moral, economic, and political reasons, to support USA domestic and foreign policies that have led to the destruction of our nation and other nations. The USA has engaged in overthrows of governments, invasions, occupations, assassinations, and other destructive creating chaos because chaos serves the purposes of cultural control and domination.

We must insist on an open public dialogue in which transparency is present. Critics must be encouraged, as non-violence is the norm for all sides. New visions of our world must be advanced and discussed. These visions must consider the complex challenges we face, and the chaos that is present. But we must also enter the numerous and profound possibilities arising from "advances" occurring in technology, and from an emerging human consciousness of our global era.

Empire requires war -- the glorification of killing, defeating, and leaving a legacy of humiliation. Remember Fallujah! Fallujah! The USA crushed the resistance using radiated weapons leaving a legacy of impaired births for generation. Christian Warfare? Messianic Democracy? No, no, no! It is *Hellelujah! Hellelujah!*

This epic battle for a city in Iraq exemplifies the timeless legacy of hatred that has been initiated and sustained by the lies of our nation's leaders at the cost of the deaths of American soldiers and Fallujah's citizens. Today the children of Fallujah pay the tragic price of our use of weapons of mass destruction -- irradiated bullets and bombs. Will they remember? Will we remember? Why does such violence continue? It continues because it serves the interests of certain groups (e.g., people, nations, businesses).

The pursuit of empire by the United States of America is an anachronistic policy. It fails to acknowledge the realities of our global era! Empire requires a militaristic mentality, and militarism creates destruction and death. It is not the American people who choose this path. Americans recognize we are victims of the concentration of power in a few. We recognize government and corporate corruption is rampant. We recognize the perpetuation of a cronyism that ties public and private paths to employment, position, and assured wealth.

Americans are tired of endless wars. Wars have drained needed funds for rebuilding our nation. Funds from endless wars are needed for building schools, clinics, and national infrastructure. Funds are needed for human services, and most of all, funds are needed to recover a sense of national decency and purpose.

Those few in positions of wealth, power, and position benefit from war; they lack conscience and regard for human suffering and death. History reveals the pursuit of empire always results in decline and collapse. Can anyone deny we are witnessing a fall from grace? We continue, as a nation, now linked to corporate and special interests, to consolidate our international national power, to exploit other people and lands, to militarize our society, and to deceive our citizens with half-truths and lies. In this tragic process, we nurture our decline. Ultimately, empire must seize total control and domination, and in the process destroy itself.

Making the "Choice:" Peace or War

The "choice" of paths is clear! Peace or War! I have summarized the choices and consequences of the paths in two tables: Destructive Foreign Policies and Actions (Table 1) and Constructive Foreign and Domestic Policies and Actions (Table 2). The options are listed alphabetically. The items are not exhaustive; others are welcome to add to the lists. Never has a fork in the road been clearer with regard to the "choice" that must be made. If we fail, we are endorsing and approving global upheaval and chaos.

Table 1:
Counter-Productive/Destructive USA Foreign and Domestic Policies, Actions, Choices, and Alternatives (Alphabetized)

- Assassinations/death squads/drones;
- Bounties for info/capture, and assassination;
- Bribery, purchase, and installation of pro-American leaders and dictators;
- Celebration of national "morality" in the face of evil acts;
- Collaboration/contracts with foreign universities, scientists, professional organizations, and intelligence agencies defaming their character;
- Contingent "humanitarian" aid – implicit and explicit;
- Contingent "foreign" aid;
- Control of UN via vetoes and economic and political pressures;
- Control of IMF and World Bank;
- Cooperation with foreign nation security services (e.g., military, intelligence, corporations);
- Development of domestic crowd controls (militarization of police);
- Drones(Widespread use of drones by domestic/national groups and agencies);
- Drug wars. Corruption of local officials;
- Disproportionate support of "allies." Enemification of others;
- Entrapments of targeted individuals and groups – persons of interest;
- Establishment of military bases [more than 700 known USA foreign bases];
- Exportation of unpopular American culture (i.e., consumerism, materialism, commodification, competition, crony capitalism, corruption, celebritization)
- False flag operations disguised military and/or economic interventions/invasions);
- Foreign student/faculty/consultant exchanges (used for intelligence recruitment);

- Fund development of disguised/pseudo-organizations used for national military and security purposes (e.g. Human Ecology Fund, ONR, AID);
- Glorification of war, militarism, warrior mentalities and images, *machismo*;
- Hegemonic globalization (i.e., control of socio-technical changes and economy);
- Infiltration of peace, anti-war groups, and social activist organizations;
- Invasion and overthrow, including regime change;
- Justification of torture ("enhanced interrogation");
- Mass surveillance, monitoring, and archiving of info/ communication data;
- Massive growth in government/private intelligence agencies and organizations;
- Media influence and control via biased news and biased news commentators;
- Military interventions and occupation of nations and regions;
- Mind control technologies (e.g., drugs, EMR, behavior control technologies);
- Negotiation/conflict resolution delays are now policy;
- No Prosecution of connected military, government, civilian law violators/abusers;
- Military occupation of foreign nations, regions, and cities;
- Promotion of nationalism, pseudo-patriotism, USA exceptionalism;
- *Project for a New American Century* (Developed to insure USA Hegemony);
- *Project Infra Guard* (Collaboration between FBI and hundreds of thousands of businesses in USA to report on citizens resulting in creation of mass list of citizens with no opportunity for contesting surveillance. (Every mall and every store provides video and other personal information;

- Propaganda to instill citizen fear, and vilification of individuals and groups;
- Recruitment of spies, informers, collaborators, agents among friends, neighbors. The best spy is a person who doesn't now they are a spy, but in fact, as they share information on neighbors, friends, and family, the information is collected and archived;
- Renditions in numerous countries;
- Use surrogate nations and forces to accomplish military goals;
- Use false-flag incidents;
- Use major philanthropic foundations to influence policy and actions;
- Vilification, demonization, enemification of domestic and/or international critics;
- Weapons/arms dealer sales for money, and for promoting conflicts;
- Witness protection programs.

Table 2:
Productive Foreign Policy and Domestic Options, Choices, Alternatives: Paths to Peace and Social Justice

- Acknowledge the national security of the USA is best secured by pursuing and modeling peace, not by engaging in constant accusations and the "enemification" of nations, cultures, religions, and people;
- Address and resolve domestic inequities and inequalities in wealth, power, and position. Create new policies for equity and opportunity;
- Address and limit monopolies (e.g., Big Agro, Big Pharm, Big Health, Big Transportation, Big Education, etc.) because these monopolies concentrate power, and they become impossible to control – "Too big to fail."
- Address the reality of USA decline in reputation and image by stopping the pursuit of a global empire;

- Adopt a "Never Again" policy and practices for all countries, by all countries. "Never again" must not be limited to a single group or nation;
- Apologize and ask for forgiveness in a public forum. Express intention to no longer pursue violence and war as national policy;
- "Be the nation you want others to be;"
- Build museums, monuments, holidays, and tributes to peace. Stop glorification of war;
- Cease all vilification of Muslims and Muslim nations;
- Condemn and prosecute apartheid;
- Choose and support non-violent and non-killing protests and social changes;
- Circulate UDHR to all schools and governments as an accepted guide;
- Close Guantanamo, and other WOT prisons, camps, and rendition sites;
- Destroy all weapons of mass destruction (Nuclear, Toxic, Gas, etc);
- Develop Department of Peace as an official standing cabinet office separate from State or Defense Departments;
- Develop a metric to assess and prosecute USA international abuses and crimes;
- Develop metrics to assess USA contributions to advancing humanity and the natural sectors. Assess metrics constantly;
- Develop, implement, and empower UN conflict resolution office;
- Develop ethic/ethos of global interdependency;
- Diplomacy dialogue, rather than military force or violent interventions;
- Educate women and children, and re-educate men;
- Empower UN, and improve its functions and roles;
- End corporate political election influence, control, and dominance;
- End global surveillance and restore privacy and constitutional rights;

- Increase governmental transparency and accountability;
- International loan forgiveness;
- Join and cooperate with international courts;
- Limit "imperial" president powers as reflected in abuses of signing statements;
- Limit lobbyist influence and control of public offices;
- Limit Presidential terms of office to six years;
- Limit Congressional terms of office to eight years. End seniority system of power;
- Limit military-industrial-congressional-education complex powers;
- Non-Contingent humanitarian aid and assistance, rather than contingent aid;
- Practice humility, apology, and forgiveness;
- Prosecute American war and military crimes to national and international laws;
- Public apology for violent and destructive national and international policies and actions (e.g. NATO);
- Reconsider political and economic treaties that isolate and marginalize nations (e.g., TPP) and seek hegemonic control (e.g., Russia, China);
- Resist military solutions to conflicts and disagreements – choose diplomacy;
- Restore balance of power across executive, congressional, and justice sectors. Dominance of the executive branch under the auspices of protecting national security has been abused, and has proven a failure and crime;
- Restorative justice to victims;
- Restrict central banking model of financial control over nations' debt;
- Review immediate and long-term consequences of DHS/NSA Abuses;
- Stop "for profit" prisons, and their associated judicial corruption;
- Speak truth, do not distort or exaggerate, practice transparency;
- Use "Justice" as an arbiter for decisions;

Some Closing Thoughts

These are **NOT** musings of an idealist! They are facts embedded in choices. There is an urgent need for new ideological foundations to replace our nation's historic reliance on war and destruction to achieve ends. Our nation's history is stained with the blood of indigenous peoples, with the blood of slavery, and with the blood of world wars whose resolutions (victories?) produced a heritage of continued reliance on military solutions and revenge from those who "lost" or from those who now see the intentions of the USA and its allies. All sides lose in war! There are no victors.

The challenges of a global era require a different approach requiring USA participation in the world, but not its domination. The world had changed. Yet the USA continues to pursue policies, strategies, and tactics that fuel war and conflict across the world. They are anachronistic! Even as national leaders speak of desires for peace, and for the intentions to help establish and support "democracies," it is apparent these are basically strategies and tactics for continuing to establish dominant political, economic, and social positions.

I have come to a fork in the road. I can see two paths before me. The path less taken is clear. Its' earth and grass are un-trodden, its greenery remains, and its horizon, distant, but visible. I love my country, amidst its' many flaws and inconsistencies. I am still proud of its noble foundations and comforts. But I can no longer accept the belief: "My country right or wrong." My country has betrayed its' promise and potential!

Imagine Gandhi, Martin Luther King Jr., Nelson Mandela, and a score of others standing at a fork in the road, and saying to you:

"Do not be afraid. Do not hesitate! Do not yield to uncertainty. If you choose the wrong path -- a path hidden in its consequences of violence, suffering, and destruction -- retrace your steps, and follow the other path. It is never too late to grasp your mistakes. Learn from your errors! Walk the path of peace. In peace, there is forgiveness and redemption for individuals, groups, nations. Choose peace not war!"

Afghanistan:
Elegy . . . Unfinished Tapestry?

Preface: I apologize to all Afghan people if my poem offends in any way. I wrote this poem reflexively following the brutal murder of a young Afghan woman, *Farkhunda Malikzada*, falsely claimed to have burned a *Koran*. I do not wish to intrude, in any way, in your individual or your country's lived experiences in pursuit of identity, security, and survival amidst continuous foreign invasions and occupations. These have resulted in suffering and death of genocidal intent and proportion. I write in sympathy, empathy, compassion, and shared hope.

I.

Afghanistan!
   Afghanistan!
      Beyond deliverance!
         Unfinished tapestry,
            Awaiting looms,
               Threads, strands, fibers,
                  Weavers!

"Stan" among "Stans:"
   Pakistan, Kazakstan, Turkmenistan, Baluchistan
      Kyrgyzstan, Tajikistan, Uiguristan, Wajiristan, Uzbekistan . . .

   Afghanistan!
      Long ago, *Pashtunistan*!
         Place, land, country, nation, people,
            Home!

Afghanistan!
  Afghanistan!
    Pashtuns, Tajiks, Hazara, Uzbeks, Kazaks,
      Aimaks, Turkmen, Uigurs, Balochs:

Intrepid warriors in turbaned *Pakols*,
  Tribal names and blood lines,
    Exotic to foreign ears and minds:
      Proud peoples:
        Human in every way:
          Vessels that bleed,
            Flesh that burns,
              Bones that dry and wither!

Fathers, sons, husbands, brothers,
  Mothers, daughters, sisters, cousins, family, friends!
    Decaying in rock piles, shallow graves, smoldering huts!
      Flesh for foragers – vermin, insects, vultures,
        Sacrificial testaments to sacrifice . . .
          Canonized names tearfully recited,
            Immutable gazes narrate history.

Branded barbaric in scripture and custom,
  Among those seeking envied geography,
    Ignorant of peaceful warrior traditions,
      Tribal loyalties,
        Village identities,
          Family ties,
            Ordered lives
              Inscribed memories!

Flag-waving invaders:
  Parades, anthems, medals, promises,
    Tanks, artillery, cadenced-stepping soldiers,
      Red coats, pith helmets,
        Camouflaged, dark glasses!

Harbingers of death,
Departing as they came,
In disbelief!
Their nation's history:
Sullied, soiled, stained!
Their soldiers:
Minds, limbs, senses – shattered.
Afghanistan remains!

II.

Afghanistan!
Afghanistan!
Strategic passage:
West to East,
East to West,
Imagined buffer for empires!

Mountains, valleys, rivers, plains,
Formidable, challenging, impassable!
Boundless contradictions!
Resilient native character,
Granite temperament,
Enduring – outliving time.

Afghanistan!
Afghanistan!
Insatiable invasions!
Beyond Shakespearean imagination!
Ravenous control!
Voracious appetites,
Unquenched avarice!

Ravaged by war!
Destroyed in resistance!
Conquest denied!

Eternal trauma,
Body, mind, seed!

Women defiled,
Foreign lives planted,
Between struggling thighs!
Entry forced,
Identity undefined.
Misery daily fare,
Smells known!
Blood, cordite, semen!

III.

Afghanistan!
Afghanistan!
Should we shout, scream,
Accept savagery,
Tolerate insult, assault, rape?

Should we speak?
With diplomatic restraint!
Deny committed sins?
Forge unholy alliances!
Sign new maps?
Defy ancient order!

"Yes, Mr. President;
Thank you Mr. Prime Minister;
It is kind of you, General!"

"Oh, that is my secretary, General;
Her family and five children lost.
She is unsure: drones, IED, bombs?
Mute now!
Sullen witness!
We have all seen so much,

For so long,
We wait!"

"We understand your concerns
For Russia, China, India, Pakistan!
Narcotics trade!
Human rights!
Terrorism!
Tactics, strategies, policies,
To contain . . ."

"We welcome your military,
We accept your apology
For Kandahar, Kabul, Herat . . . !"
Please, Sir, allow me:
*Have you tasted, "***Qabili Palau?***"*
Our "national" dish!
Do you like lamb?

In silence:
"We are caught!
East-West balancing act!
Ancient customs!
Tribal rivalries!
Sunni-Shia hatreds!
War-lord ambitions!
Revenge required!
Life, death . . . . "

IV.

Afghanistan!
Afghanistan!
Sacrificial lamb for the world!
Bleating!
Bleeding!

Centuries lost,
Cultures destroyed.

Reached by Alexander the Great,
Megos Alexandros;
Macedonian legacy?
Generations of green eyes!

Silk Road passage,
Khyber Pass!
Mythic place for Kipling's tales,
Victoria's gift to Britain's people!
Borders, demarcations, sovereignty!

England's legacy?
Debate for a nation's conscience:
Gladstone lectured rapacious Disraeli:

> *"Remember the rights of the savage. . . . Remember the sanctity of life in the hill villages of Afghanistan, among the winter snows, is as inviolable in the eyes of Almighty God as can be your own."*

England's legacy?
Conscience!
Sublimated guilt with arrogance!
A new word for armies: "Sanctity."
Eager to continue
Messianic missions:
"Take up the White man's burden."

A "Great Game" -- played without native consent!
A ravenous game for nations:
Britain, Russia, Germany, India, Pakistan.
Prize for Queen, Czar, Raj, Kaiser, Ministers, Presidents!

Imperialism's darkest hours,
Unfinished!
Awaiting America!
But first: **"Empire!"**

Boundaries fashioned under duress!
Durand Line! 1893!
Sir Mortimer Durand,
British India diplomat,
Skilled in deceit.

Tea at Parachinar!
"May I remind you:"
"You really have no choice!"

A new Northwest-Frontier Province:
Harsh reality soothed by tea!
Abdur Raman Khan,
Afghan Amir,
Compliant, impressionable, malleable!
Pretense at face!
"We can accept this line."

Treaty -- written in English -- signed!
"You do, *Amir Khan*, understand our decision?
"We look forward, Minister Durand,
To an era of mutual cooperation!
All will benefit!"

Pashtuns . . . Balochs . . . warrior tribes!
Division essential:
Northwest area must be separated.
"Security of India!"
"Jewel in the Crown!"
"More tea?"
"Two or one?"

Afghanistan!
   Afghanistan!
      A nation, people, history sacrificed!
        Beseeching victim!
          Splayed on altars,
            For wealth, power, position.
          Illusions of empire!

Soviet Union – USSR – invasion:
   Modern arms, ideological intention;
      Aspirations! Delusions! Hallucinations!
      Nine years, 1 month, 3 weeks, 1 day.

In response: America arms *Mujahadeen*!
   Communism must be stopped!
      Al Q'aida born!
        ISIS nurtured!
          Taliban required!
        Hatred sired!

Cold wars spill blood:
   Victims of grand designs!
      Millions in dead!
        Millions refugees, displaced!
          Faces, now statistics!
            Collateral damage!

Amid upheaval,
   New powers emerge:
      Warlords, religious zealots, village chiefs, foreign forces!
        "Who is in charge here?"
          "I am!"
          "Who are you?"

Soviet legacy?
   Humiliation!
      Accusation!

Defiled name!
Satanic nation!

America?
Coalition, consortium, confederation . . .
Conspiracy of the *"Willing,"*
Conscienceless term: *"Willing!"*
NATO!
Code for death and destruction!
Demoncracy!

V.

Afghanistan!
Afghanistan!
"America's troops will remain and help!"
Centuries dismissed . . . with impunity,
Tribal inheritances insulted!
Local ways ridiculed,
Traditions . . . crushed
What savage God . . .
Ordained you, savior?

Afghanistan!
Afghanistan!
Decay, decline, lawless!
Men, women, children,
Villages, earth, fields -- fodder!
Imperfect resurrection!

America's legacy:
Purveyor of sullied fruit!
Unrepentant!
Apologies?
"Our intentions were good!"
Expressions of guilt impossible!
Semblance of villainy denied!

"Never say you are sorry!
　　Never say you made a mistake!
　　　Never question our rationale!
　　　　How could you explain
　　　　　To limbless soldiers,
　　　　　　Media, taxpayers, lawyers?
　　　　　　　Vietnam, Iraq, Afghanistan!
　　　　　　　Tolerance is gone!"

Colonialism, imperialism, capitalism,
　　Corruption, opium, slavery, prostitution!
　　　Choose your "Cides:"
　　　　Ecocides, fraticides, infanticides
　　　　Suicides,
　　　　　Genocides!
　　　　　Afghanicide!
　　　　　　Noun! Verb!

VI.

To all coveting this fabled land,
　　I say:
　　　Fall on your knees!
　　　　Beg forgiveness.
　　　　　Pray to the god of your choice,
　　　　　　Beat your chest for penance.
　　　　　　Shed tears.
　　　　　　　Renounce violence!

Behold your tainted tracks!
　　"Civilized?"
　　　An unfitting word!
　　　　"Barbarous" more apt!
　　　　What lesson remains?
　　　　　. . . . Rashkalnikov!

Commentary:

Afghanistan: history, country, people, culture, a difficult topic to confine to poetic words. How does one share imprints of a people, land, or nation, torn by endless periods of social upheaval, destruction, death -- victim of its own and of foreign hands? Understanding legacy is essential, yet insufficient!

An elegy is a sad poem – a poem expressing sorrow, grief, and longing for someone who is dead or dying. Many would say the term "elegy" is premature. They claim Afghanistan has survived numerous invasions and occupations by foreign powers and internal regime changes. Yet, Afghanistan remains! This is true! But what Afghanistan remains?

Borders are erased, new boundaries accepted! Nations emerge and disappear, even as remnants of cultures remain. People assume new faces and bodies. This is history! A story well-known in Central Asia! Revisionist map-makers omnipresent, eager to display old and new lines – latitudes and longitudes!

I offer a second sub-title in this poem: **"Unfinished Tapestry,"** hoping Afghanistan may find stability and security among its own weavers and looms. The tapestry metaphor was gleaned from the words of the talented poet, Edna St. Vincent Millay, in her published sonnet, *Huntsman, What Quarry?* Afghanistan's looms have proven inadequate; its prior weavers unwilling to accept their tattered failures, continuing to weave with soiled hands, torn threads, and broken looms.

I offer this poem to Afghanistan with apologies. Nothing can heal loss, grief, and sorrow – a decimated population, a denied national identity, a future uncertain. I apologize for all who should, and do not!

Can Afghanistan's destiny be shaped by its own hand? I know only no permanent solution can be found in violence and war. Choices define futures! Can an "Unfinished Tapestry" find healing, peace, dignity? I do not know! Until such time, as South African Bishop Tutu said amidst his country's darkest hours: *"We remain prisoners of hope."*

PASHTUN WOMAN:
Enduring the Unendurable

I.

I must now leave this land I love,
Or perish, and remain forever.

I will miss blue skies high above,
Mountains, valleys, rivers, I have wandered.

There is no reason to remain,
All life and memory now deeply stained.

They said they came to make us free,
But all they brought was misery.

I must make a sacred journey from my home,
Seek life anew far from where I was born.

My heart and spirit are now broken and forlorn,
Buried, forever, in earth scorched and torn!

II.

I will join others for a distant walk,
They say they know where they are going.

They say their brothers have gone before.
And there found safety from the war.

They whisper *Peshawar* many times,
I will follow them, but perhaps there die.

My eyes are swollen from my tears,
I travel blindly, no longer feeling fear.

**Soldiers and warriors promised us peace,
And so much more!**

**But they were only here
To make a war!**

**Their words were lies, absent any sincere meaning,
Our bodies now lie dead and bleeding.**

III.

What did my tiny children do?
They were so innocent as they played.

They brought us joy and laughter,
Now I place flowers on their graves.

My husband is gone, no longer here,
Buried beneath rubble and rocks I fear.

He said he must go to fight the foe.
It was written he said, so it must be so.

**Now I pack soiled sour grains to eat,
Tie my strongest sandals on my feet.**

**I carry now my few remains,
Tattered photos covered with blood stains.**

IV.

Do they know or care what they have done?
With their lies and promises, what have they won!

They have planted endless grief,
The war they cause will never cease.

We are *Pashtun*, brave and strong,
But now all we have left are poems and song.

I go now to close the gate,
I go now, to follow fate.

Comment:

The words to this lyrical poem, **Pashtun Woman,** are presented in a rhythm and evocative cadence to the delicate and haunting melody, **A Thousand Splendid Suns**. This melody was composed by the talented Australian folk-song writer, singer, and diplomat, Iian "Fred" Smith. The singing is by gifted Australian songstress, Liz Frencham. The title of this melody was adapted from a Seventeenth-Century Afghan poem, written by **Saib e Tabrizi**. The version in my possession was sung at the **Concert for Uruzgan,** at the Burrinja Cultural Centre, Sydney, Australia, on June 19, 2014.

The website for Mr. Smith is: **www.fredsmith.com.au.** I am indebted to Mr. Smith and Ms. Frencham, for doing more to alert us to the horrors of the endless Afghan war, than all the news printed or spoken by politicians and panderers.

More Comments

Estimates of the number of Afghan refugees are difficult to determine with exactness. International authorities conclude there are more than six million Afghani refugees and internally displaced persons. Most of this number of refugees and displaced people traveled to Iran and to Pakistan, many settled amidst uncertainty and deprivation in the town of Peshawar, Pakistan.

The full extent of their plight in these countries is often unknown. They are unwanted and subject to abuse and exploitation. While Afghan *diaspora* exist across the world, many finding new lives in Europe or the United States, the number finding safety is low, and the world seems to have ignored their plight. It is, in many ways, genocide, of the Afghan people, a genocide rooted in abandonment and powerlessness at the hands of hegemonic powers.

And still the USA and its NATO allies insist on remaining in Afghanistan with promises of humanitarian aid, and vocal support from a puppet Afghanistan government. The scenario is now well known. It has been used by the USA scores of times, at the expense of the lives and wellbeing of a nation's citizens.

The scenario: Overthrow and existing government alien to USA and NATO agendas. Establish a puppet government. Make financial payoffs to the leaders of the puppet government, and gradually insert troops under the guise of assisting to train a local army, and to reconstruct a nation.

No where! No where, has this policy, strategy, and tactic proven more devastating than in Afghanistan. The death and destruction has proven endless; and the USA military occupation and war in Afghanistan, is now considered endless. Why? Ask the refugees! Ask the USA military/industrial complex! Humanitarian agencies may say it is the position of this ancient land, a bridge – the Khyber Pass connection between Afghanistan and Pakistan, connecting the Capitol of Kabul with Peshawar.

Afghanistan is bordered by Iran, Turkmenistan Kyrghistan, and Pakistan – a "Stan" amidst "Stans'." Afghanistan is strategically located. Strategic for whom, and for what purposes! Afghanistan is a pawn in the global game of world order, in which hegemonic powers struggle for ascendancy and control at the cost of human lives and suffering. Afghanistan is a buffer for the West. China and Russia loom on the other side.

I have often wondered, is the war about the heroin-addiction industry – crime cartels and nations seeking power and position? It is said 90% of the world's opium is grown in Afghanistan. It is alleged Taliban forces, exacting tolls religious fanaticism, ended opium production, while the presence of United States and NATO occupation increased this percentage. There is too much money to be made by nations and cartels to yield control. Shame! Recall the weapons for drugs in Central America, and the drugs on the streets of LA!

PAX ROMANA

I.

Months in the warm Sicilian sun
　　Have bronzed my skin!
　　　　Walks in lemon groves have cleared my lungs.
　　　　　　Salty waters of the *Mare Internum*
　　　　　　　　Have cleansed my body and limbs,
　　　　　　　　　　Lifting the blood and stains of battle!

But neither sun, nor sea, or seasons' change,
　　Can release the memories from the Northern Campaign!
　　　　There, on unyielding earth,
　　　　　　On rock and ice,
　　　　　　　　Amidst howling winds,
　　　　　　　　　　Numbed senses and thought,
　　　　　　　　　　　　I fought for you, Rome.

II.

No ordered ranks of disciplined soldiers
　　Marching to meet us!
　　　　No siege of towns and villages
　　　　　　Ending in surrender,
　　　　　　　　Yielding at our sight!

This battle knew no limits,
　　A savage struggle -- sword, ax, and spear,
　　　　Shattered shields,
　　　　　　Cleaved armor,
　　　　　　　　Earth bathed in blood.

They did not flee our
  Mighty legions, Rome!
    These men of the North
      Did not tremble before our crimson and gold banners!

They did not run from our horse cavalry,
  Nor from our ordered ranks,
    Our beating rhythmic drums,
      Blaring horns,
        Shouted commands!

These were tall, massive men,
  Screaming names of their Gods,
    As they threw themselves upon us!
      Their eyes wide,
        Nostrils flaring,
          Untamed and braided hair,
            Bear and deer for clothing!

Their weapons: iron, wood, and hide . . .
  And courage,
    Born of contempt for our cause!

In death, they were unbowed,
  Shrieking as swords and spears
    Pierced throats,
      Axes slashed limb and head from body.

III.

We won, Rome,
  As we have before.
    But beware, Rome.

Barbarians have been kept from our gates.
  Our borders stretch to new lands,
    New outposts now rise beyond distant mountains.

Once again, Rome, citizens sing your praises,
    Senators speak of your noble aims,
        Poets write of your might,
            Slaves serve your needs.

For yet another time,
    People in distant lands
        Yield to your will,
            Cower in awe at your power, wealth, and presence.

For this, tens of thousands died in pain and suffering,
    Heaped in tortured postures
        On blood soaked land,
            Flesh for crows.

For this, steeds died in agony,
    Rising on shattered legs,
        Entrails scattered darkened earth,
            Villages sacked and burned,
                Women raped,
                    Men tortured,
                        Children enslaved.

IV.

Heed me, Rome!
    Nothing more remains for us to conquer,
        To subdue,
            To quench our lust for more!

Test no more your might
    Against the men of the North
        -- Germania, Scandia, Anglia.
            Turn now to that within our minds and spirits.
                Heal rifts and needs.
                    Make right your own, Rome.

V.

Ask me not to fight further,
 If still you yearn and long for more!
  If you crave war,
   Send others,
    Those youth who favor you still!

Or send mercenaries,
 Paid with stained gold,
  Grateful for bitter wine and sour bread,
   A chance for adventure,
    Told to by dishonest men,
     Round shadowy home fires!

I am weary,
 Deaf to siren songs!
  I have buried sword, shield, armor,
   Beneath an olive tree,
    Standing upon a hill,
     Apart from the others!

I seek no longer the camaraderie of camp fires,
 Noble horses, champing, eager for battle,
  Tents, maps, marches,
   Bonds with trusted men!

My face is lined,
 My limbs ache,
  I want the comforts of routine,
   The solace of silence,
    The peace of a morning sun,
     Or a rising moon!
      The gentle touch of a woman!

Call on me no more, Hadrian.
 I have given all I had to Rome,

> Only sullied and stained life remains,
> A tortured mind,
> A damaged spirit!

Comment:

I wrote the first draft of this poem on June 10, 1987, as I was writing a historical fiction novel that took me back to ancient Rome. I completed a second draft on June 15, 1987: 8:45-9:05 PM. Other drafts followed as I continued to find a meaning in the anti-war and anti-empire sentiment. I wrote yet another draft on June 27, 2012, as I found myself saddened by the wars and violence in Iraq and Afghanistan. I completed this version on March 26, 2013, aware, more than ever before, of the wars dominating human life across the ages, and continuing to exact a brutal toll on all sides.

Life and Love

- Cosmic Alchemy
- On Love in the Afternoon, and More…
- "You Have Made a Rose…"
- I Dream Too, Yah Know!
- Hands

Cosmic Alchemy

You are woman,

    I am man.

You are north,

    I am south.

You are winter and spring,

    I am summer and fall.

You are earth and water,

    I am fire and wind.

You are eternity,

    I am time.

You are moon,

    I am sun.

We are one!

Comment:

I wrote this poem on June 15, 1989. It was a difficult period in my life. I had just resigned as the Senior Vice President for Academic Affairs at the University of Hawaii, Honolulu, Hawaii. Amidst the turmoil I experienced and witnessed, the sullying and staining of academia, and so much more, I sought meaning in "love" itself; yet this too seemed insufficient. Ultimately, I understood what I craved was intimacy, union, connection, bonding, a moving beyond opposites, toward oneness. This impulse, this effort, after "intimacy," remains with me. It is a "cosmic" alchemy.

On Love in the Afternoon, and More . . .
(Fiction)

She looked at me, with her usual innocence, a source of vul-
nerability in others, but in her, a paradoxical source of strength. Her
ingenuous, transparency, and openness, revealed a disposition, a
temperament, a character of uncompromising goodness -- a virtue
not to be defiled.

"So what is it?" she asked. **"And why is it so good?"**

Her lack of knowledge of *Chambord* did not faze her. In others,
such a lack would be a silent shame. I can hear them say: "I should
know that, I even lived in France. But I don't know it," they would
say sheepishly.

Not her! Things were to be known, when they needed to be known,
and then they were to be grasped and embraced with an understanding
exceeding words. She knew with all her senses, and this gave her a
mystique at once attractive and bewildering.

"Ahhh, Chambord," I said. **"How can I describe it to you?"**

I gathered my thoughts and said: **"Well first the facts. Then I
will tell you more about the magic of Chambord."**

She looked up at me! Tilted her head slightly! Raised her eyebrows
ever so slightly, still trusting my words.

I had her attention! I had not yet, however, captured her imagination,
an imagination I knew was filled with wondrous thoughts, and ways

of knowing, making her alive in each moment, filled with interest of the world, yet willing to remain apart . . . to refrain from the ordinary.

She possessed a reflexive way of keeping the world from sullying her way-of-being, yet a willingness to test its attractions. There was a delicate selective detachment!

I relished my role as a source of knowledge for her because of her genuine interest in knowing, not so much for using knowledge, but for the sheer delight of knowing – like a young child who asks earnestly of her mother as they walk: "Why is the grass green?"

"Chambord is a French black and red raspberry liqueur," I said. **"It was originally made in the Loire Valley, France, in the 17th century. It acquired a special reputation when Louis XIV visited the Chambord Castle in the area, and delighted in its taste. In time, it became associated with royalty -- a special liqueur."**

She continued to stare at me, saying nothing. Looking! Waiting! Wanting more! Content to let the course of my words proceed to their inevitable end, an answer to the question she had asked: **"So what is it, and why is it so good?"**

"Today," I continued, **"Chambord is the proprietary product of a large American company. The company is located in Kentucky. But do not let the company's location, admittedly less exotic and lacking the obvious *savor faire* of France, detract from Chambord itself,"** I said with a grin.

She smiled, acknowledging my efforts after dark humor and wit. Even as I spoke the words, I felt I offered her nothing of value. It was as if my descriptions, and evaluative efforts, designed to reveal my knowledge and wit were unnecessary.

She did not need dark humor, sarcasm, or pretense. These did not feed her nature, nor comfort or seduce her. It was as if she recognized and understood the folly of excess, and the hidden malice so often present in words.

There was purity about her. I had asked myself many times before: Is it possible to meet a human being whose nature is unsullied and unmarred by the world in which we lived? Someone pristine and untouched in her nature, not subject to the subtle or obvious wiles of confusion and abuse as society pursues its control of our lives.

I recalled the words of the Rousseau-era romanticist poet who described the meeting of an 18th Century indigenous chief from the new land of America who had been taken from to be shown to the crown heads of Europe for the purposes of theater.

The poet had described the moment when the "noble savage" walked toward the King: *"In Ataliba's pure unsullied mind, loomed the pure offspring of the heart."* It was not **Ataliba** had no culture, but rather his culture carried with it a way-of-being in the world in harmony with life. It was not distorted by excess.

I thought to myself, she fits Rousseau's romanticist notions about the beauty of simplicity, the nobility of the unadorned, and the timeless virtue of purity. I paused to collect my thoughts, and then proceeded to share more facts about Chambord.

"Chambord, today, is made from black and red raspberries, some exotic imported vanilla, some North African citrus peel, some honey, and cognac – it is 16.5% alcohol by the time it is placed in its regal round bottle with a royalty crown on top. By the time of its final processing, it is a deep-dark burgundy color. Most experts consider Chambord, to be a "top-shelf" or a "top-tier" liqueur."

I did not know if she understood this talk of "alcohol" -- jargon of bars, sophisticates, caught in the latest fads, needing to be "in." I understood in that moment an essential difference between men and women – the source of so much gender discord.

Men want and seek information: facts – details -- minutiae. It is a source of power for them -- to know the "realities" of an object or situation so they may act with decisiveness and confidence.

Women, I understood, seek something more than facts. They find value in the nuances of feelings revealed by facts. A fact is more than a fact for a woman. It embodies a meaning, and meaning requires emotion, and emotion is a way-of-being in the world.

In that moment, I understood the beauty of the Eastern distinction, the harmony of *Yin* and *Yang,* a fusing of male and female, and yet, their separation.

In her presence, my mind was alive! That was her gift! She was like a unpainted canvas for an artist, whose very absence of content gave the artist a chance to imagine, to play with possibilities of what could be done before touched by a brush.

In her presence, my mind was free! I stopped my reverie, my enchantment, and returned to the task, staring at her now with a new sense of enjoying the moment. Ah, communication! Sharing each other!

"Even when you first see the bottle," I said, **"Chambord, excites the senses."**

She smiled, and asked: **"All the senses?"**

"Yes!" I replied: **"All the senses!"**

Then, trying to introduce levity, I said: **"Like when you see Catherine Deneuve. Not Bardot, but Deneuve. All of the senses are aroused. "At least for me, that is the case."**

I tried to regain my composure, touching my chest, and clearing my throat.

"Deneuve is Chambord, Bardot is Scotch. They are both beautiful, but in different ways."

The more I tried, the more I seemed to add confusion to what I wanted to say, and to be, in her eyes; someone she would welcome into her life. I did not want to be a necessity for her – necessities only hurt. But someone whose presence she would find to be . . . enjoyable, enriching! I searched for words, sacred words."

"When one sips Chambord," I said, **"following the usual rituals of looking at its color in a small crystal cognac glass, smelling its fragrance, swirling it a bit, and then letting it touch your lips. At that moment, you know you are on the verge of a special experience."**

"It is simultaneously sweet," I said softly, now aware my words were detracting from the magic of the moment, **"with a touch of bitter; mellow yet aromatic; delicate, yet determined to remain with you, long after you have sipped it, and inhaled the first breath."**

"As it passes your tongue, and moves within your mouth, and you swallow gently, you become aware it is an experience needing no other accompaniment, no cheese, no pate, or fruit. It is an experience unto itself."

I wanted to say: **"Like you!"** I was becoming heady with my own words, her presence, and her silence.

"I should add, however, I feel it could benefit from the presence of another, if only to share the wonder of the moment."

"Yes," I said quickly to resolve all doubt: **"Chambord is best when the moment is shared."**

I looked at her to grasp her response to my long reply! I wondered whether my detailed efforts at description had dulled her interest. Words, words, words, they can be magic, or they can close minds.

"Well," I said, **"That is Chambord! Does my reply answer your question?**

"Forgive me! I may have said more than is necessary. I am sorry. I am a professor; given a chance, I add complexity! It is the professor's sin." I said with a hint of being contrite.

She smiled and looked at me. Her head tilted slightly as she brushed away her hair. She looked at me from the top of her eyes.

"Thank you," she said. "I understand."

"I think what you were saying . . . is Chambord . . . is like . . . like making . . . love in the afternoon!"

Comment:

I do not understand the source of this story, first written on February 3, 2014. Was, it once again, that special quest for finding beauty in person, time, and place . . . in objects about us taken for granted, even as they offer pleasure.

It is as if life gifts us with senses to behold the beauty about us, challenging us to become conscious of the possibilities. *Je nais c'est pais! C'est la vie! Magnifique!*

"You Have Made a Rose . . ."

Preface:

This is a short story; a fictional account of a brief meeting with an imagined friend, Carol, a middle-aged mother of a 16-year-old daughter, Becky, diagnosed with autism.

Autism is a bewildering disorder of unknown etiology. Today, autism is spoken of as a spectrum of disorders, encompassing individuals requiring constant care for basic needs, to individuals with highly specialized talents and skills placing them in genius level functioning (e.g., Asperger's Syndrome; *savants*).

In the extremes, are many individuals with IQs ranging between 50-75 scores. The scores indicate they are educable; however they require specialized schooling and training, sufficient to develop daily-life skills. Adult supervision and guidance are typically required.

The adolescent period is a difficult one for educable youth diagnosed with autism. Indeed, adolescence is difficult for all children as biological, psychological, and social changes cascade into one another in a period German's call *Sturm und Drang.* This phrase an be loosely translated as *"Storm and Longing.*

It is a good phrase, capturing not only the emotional turmoil, but the "longing," a state of wanting something, needing something, but not often knowing what it may be. There is a tumultuous search for satisfaction and resolution, often times dominated by uncontrolled impulses.

For youth considered autistic, adolescence is a near constant period of contention with parents, friends, and society. The assertion of their needs and impulses runs into endless impositions of controls and discipline in response to their rebellious anger and explosive outbursts, protests, and oppositional behavior. Sexual impulses are often a major source of problems, as hormonal chemistry changes seek satisfaction amid chaotic social relations.

As a clinical psychologist specializing in severe mental disorders, I had encountered a number of individuals diagnosed as autistic during practice. Meeting these individuals and their families for clinical purposes frequently required me to assume an unfortunate professional detachment. I did, however, have the opportunity to encounter a "autistic" adolescent girl, Becky, and her mother, Carol, in a more natural social setting. I had become friends with Carol, and she invited me to meet Becky.

It was a "changer" for me. It was a human encounter, unimpeded by evaluations and judgments designed to reach clinical decisions. It was enlightening! The following short story is fictional, but it is rooted in my real-life experiences. I have written the story as a letter to Carol, following my meeting Becky.

Letter to Carol

Dear Carol:

I do not know why, but I suddenly had this powerful and relentless impulse to write you the words that follow. I wrote the words non-stop -- in one session, between the 10:00 – 11:45 AM. I added a few more around 3:15 PM. The words came effortlessly, almost as if the words had been written before; some call this "magic writing."

When I finished writing at 11:45, I decided to write a preface, so you may know, as I know you will, my words may serve my needs, far more than yours or Becky's. If my words represent a reality distant and detached from the world in which you and Becky live, then know I apologize from my heart.

I would not hurt you in any way. It does not have to be real. The words can be a fictional account, a short story, perhaps a fable, or perhaps the beginning of a longer story.

I do not know, nor understand, the source of these words. I write daily: scientific and professional articles, socio-political commentaries and blogs, poetry, short stories, and any other genre linked to words. I was driven to understand, autism, beyond text-book knowledge.

I live each moment deeply, experiencing both the moment, and the flow into other moments, a life stream. I share these moments with you now for reasons I do not understand, yet I know, somehow, there is an effort after connection.

Short Story

Carol was hesitant as she led me into the living room to meet her daughter. She took a deep breath, and expelled with it a sigh, to refresh, and to make her strong amidst the uncertainty of what might occur. Carol was worried both about what I would say when I met Becky, and what Becky would say in return. She was also worried about how she would respond to both of us. The situation was delicate in so many ways. And yet, when Carol heard my words, she relaxed and smiled, and looked at Becky. Becky returned her smile.

"You have made a rose!" I said these words immediately to Carol, as I beheld Becky.

Thank you! Becky said, smiling.

But why do you think I am a rose? Becky's quick reply and question surprised Carol, but brought a smile of amazement to her face, and a shrugged shoulder response. Becky was like that for Carol, always giving unanticipated and unexpected responses.

In a brief moment, Becky showed the years of attention and love Carol had given to her, the countless hours practicing how to behave in different situations. Carol had made countless efforts to explain to Becky why Becky was who she was, and how she got that way.

Carol vacillated between protection, and the need to give Becky a chance to live her life free of Carol's presence, learning from the experience itself. Carol knew experience would often prove harsh. She knew, also, she had to let go, and one day, Becky would know both joy and sorrow, apart from Carol's presence.

"I think you are a rose because you have both inner beauty and outer beauty," I said.

Carol was silent; she felt her heart begin to race. Where would this conversation go? What should she do?

"How can you see my inner beauty, if it is inside me?" Becky asked, confident in her logic.

"When there is inner beauty, it shines out like the sun; it radiates from within, and becomes part of a person's presence. It becomes visible!"

I was hesitant as I said the last words, concerned they would not be understandable to Becky. I continued.

"A rose unfolds slowly, each petal blossoming, only to be replaced by another, until it is in full bloom. It blossoms from within."

I felt I should stop my words, and wait for Becky's response.

"Do you know I have autism?" Becky exclaimed!

"Yes, I know. Your mother shared that with me."

"Do you know what causes autism?"

"Yes and "no!" I began to gather thoughts from my clinical lectures in preparation for a reply.

"Are you a doctor? Tell me what you know, and I will tell you what I know."

"Yes, I am a doctor, and I will tell you what I know. But do not be disappointed with me if I cannot answer your questions."

Carol was silent -- both amazed and bewildered about what was occurring. She wanted to speak, to say something, but it was as if she knew she must not interfere, and must let the conversation proceed. Her thoughts raced. She concluded she trusted and loved both people. Only good could come of their meeting.

"Autism is a word. It has many meanings. We use the word a great deal in schools, clinics, hospitals, and homes. But it is used so many times, by so many people, in so many different ways we become confused, even as we use it."

"I know what it means! It means I have a problem that began long ago – probably from I was born. I do not think or act like others children because of the problem. I can't do all the things they do, but I can do things they cannot do."

"Yes, I agree with what you say."

"I have trouble reading, but I dream of amazing things; and I feel what others feel, even though I may not show it. It is a problem. But it is not always a problem."

"Yes, some people call autism a problem. It is a word we use for a group of problems with different causes."

I almost used the word "spectrum," but held back because I did not know if Becky would understand.

"Becky knows the word "spectrum," Carol interjected. **"I have explained it to her."** Carol was trying to smooth things along. There was no need.

"Oh Mom, relax. I know a lot of words. After all, you taught me. My mother is a good teacher."

"Okay! I will try to answer your question," I said.

"I think it is possible for someone diagnosed with autism to be a rose." I looked at Becky trying to see if she was following my remarks. **It is also possible to be many things. There are many types of autism."**

"But tell me what you think caused my autism, my "rose" autism?"

Carol inhaled again, waiting for my reply. She had learned people with good intentions could cause problems.

"When children grow within their mother, before they are born, so many things must occur at just the right time, and in just the right place."

"So does that mean I had the wrong things occur at the wrong time?"

"No. It does not. There are many different kinds of autism. Each person with autism is unique, each one has a different way of being and behaving, because causes vary."

I looked down, and then raised my head to look at Becky. Becky was following my words, but I knew had only little time because of attention changes.

"Okay!" I looked at Becky. She was still staring at me.

"Let me give you the quick version of a long lecture I give to my students in college." Becky smiled! Carol smiled! I smiled!

"I might go to college one day when I get older. Maybe you can be my teacher. I dream too, just like other kids."

Perhaps I should have responded to her comment. It is always best to acknowledge where someone is, rather than pursuing your own course. I continued:

"Along the way, during the time we are conceived and born, and after, many things occur. It is possible, at certain times, when your mother was caring you in her tummy, she ..."

"You mean her womb. I know that word too!"

"And I know what conceive means, too!"

"Yes! In her womb, things can occur causing a problem. Most often, it takes nine months from the time a child is conceived, to the child's birth. At different times in the nine months, things must occur in just the right order."

"Just like baking a cake! Just follow the recipe, and it will turn out okay," Becky said, as she moved her hands in a circular stirring motion.

"Sometimes thing go wrong. The recipe isn't followed."

Then what happens? Becky asked quickly. It was as if she knew the next words, but wanted to be sure of them.

"If that happens, a child's brain and nervous system can be changed. Injured! The change can make a child behave in different ways. They do some things, but not others."

"Mom said that football players can get injured from the tackling. It hurts their heads. Then when they get older, the injury shows itself."

"I am a cheer leader at my special school. I don't play football. That is for the boys."

Carol was about to interrupt. She had not used the word "injured," and she was concerned it would make Becky confused.

"Would you like some cookies I made?"

I stopped speaking.

"Yes, I would love some cookies you have made. What kind of cookies are they?"

"They are sugar cookies, but without sugar, because sugar makes me upset. I get too active. I have to be careful what I eat."

Becky jumped up, and ran to the kitchen.

Carol stared at me. **"Whew!" "Wow!" I didn't know what to say or do? I love her so much, and I always want her to be happy. I know that is not always possible. But when I see her before me, and I think of what she has gone through, my heart aches for her. I want to protect her all the time.**

Tears came to the corners of Carol's gray-green eyes.

"We will talk again. You know autism -- whatever that is -- has many causes, many dysfunctions, and many strengths. I don't want you to blame yourself. Just for the record, Becky's condition may have a thousand causes."

For example, the hormone "oxytocin" may be involved, but this does not mean all autistic children are "oxytocin-deprived."

"Forgive me! I am just an old professor. I start and can't stop."

"I hope there is "oxytocin" in the cookies, so I stop talking."

Carol smiled!

"Thanks. I can see you care, and I appreciate your words. You are kind, and have a tender heart. I have spent so much time trying to understand why. I have never come to an answer, something I might be able to tell Becky one day as she begins to ask me questions, just like she asked you. It is still a maze! All I can do is love her, and let her know she is loved by so many.

Becky returned carrying a plate of cookies. She had brought some napkins.

"I can't make tea or coffee yet. But I will learn to do that. I can pour you some milk if you want some."

"Thank you, Becky, the cookies look delicious."

"I have another question for you," Becky said: Some roses have thorns? If they do, then they have something that can hurt?"

"Hmm! That is a good question. I have a good answer. Roses have thorns, and thorns can hurt if you touch the rose in the wrong way. Thorns are there to protect the rose. The rose and thorns grow together: beauty and guardians."

"It is that way for many things, Becky. As you grow, there are people who protect you. Thorns are part of the rose, and the rose brings beauty to the thorns."

Becky smiled, and ran off. "I have to read now. See you later. Hope you like the cookies."

I stared at Carol. There were tears in her eyes.

"You are a wonderful mother, Carol. I can see your love for Becky."

I paused for a moment!

"Carol! "It takes a rose, to give birth to another rose."

Retrospect:

I was changed by my encounter with Becky. I had to confront myself as a professional and a person. I understood how professional roles distance us from human encounters. Becky and Carol made me a rose! I never want to forget the magnificence of that possibility.

I DREAM TOO, YAH KNOW!
Pour Becky

I.

I dream too, yah know!

I dream of being a cheerleader,
    Cheering before a huge crowd!

I dream of having a boy friend I love,
    And who loves me, and we kiss!

I dream of being married, and having kids,
    And loving them,
        Just like my mother loves me.
        I would be a good mom!

I dream of going to college,
    And wearing a college sweatshirt,
        Of walking across a beautiful campus,
        Filled with trees and students!
        And I feel like I belong!

Sometimes I dream I can speak French,
    And I am in Paris!
        And I am sitting in a café,
        Drinking a glass of *vin rouge!*
        That's red wine!

II.

I have good dreams and bad dreams, yah know,
    Just like you!

Sometimes I dream I am lost,
    And don't know what to do,
        And I wake up crying,
           And sobbing, and run to my mom,
        And she hugs me,
          And she tells me:
             "It was only a dream!"

But sometimes my dreams,
    Seem so real!
      It's just like I am there!

Sometimes I dream of taking a test,
    And I am not able to understand it,
      Or to answer the questions!
        And I don't know what to do!

Sometimes I dream of things that happened to me,
    Kids calling me names,
      And teasing me!
        Pushing me down!

Sometimes I dream a guardian angel,
    Will come to me at night,
      While I am sleeping,
        And will awaken me,
          And tell me I have wings,
        And I can fly.

Sometimes I dream of being happy,
    And having my family

All together,
>And they ask me to say grace at dinner.

Sometimes I dream my brother, Ben,
>Gets well,
>>And he can be just like other kids,
>>And we live together!
>>>And we play tag!

III.

I dream just like you!
>Just because I have a disorder,
>>Doesn't mean I don't dream!

I know I am autistic,
>But I also know,
>>I feel good things and bad,
>>>Just like you!

I dream, too!
>Don't think I do not!

I do!

Comment:

Pour Becky, et tout les reve et reveries!

Hands

Gripping, holding, grasping, clasping,

Throwing, opening, feeling, yielding.

Crossing lines, crinkled skin,

Hardened ridges, translucent skin.

Allaying . . . Betraying,

Revealing . . . Concealing,

Balancing . . . Weighing,

Judging . . . Playing.

Lying flat, palm side down,

Crunched in a ball,

Warped in a frown,

Folded in prayer,

Touching a child,

Parting earth,

Enduring a trial.

Your hands are you!

What you have done!

What you have been!

Your hands are your future,

Surrounded by skin!

Comment:

I wrote this poem on an airplane flight. I had placed my tray down and saw my hands before me in a new light. It was as if noticed my hands for the first time.

There before me, these magnificent hands we take for granted because they are always there for us. I wanted to honor them with poetic words, lifting them in my mind to a new status. And so this paean!

Time and Mortality Encounters

Sing me a Song in Gaelic

Sing me a song in Gaelic,
    With sweet dulcimer chords.
      Let me close my eyes and imagine,
        A glowing hearth,
          The smell of earth and wood,
            A gathering circle.

Sing me a song in Gaelic,
    Let me imagine a rhythmic drum,
      A bard's ancient chant,
        Maidens in white linen,
          Plaid kilts and scarves,
            Druids and oak groves,
              Mysteries of land and sky!

Sing me a song in Gaelic,
    Return me to times of poets, heroes, and seers,
      Undaunted warriors riding naked into battle,
        Bodies covered in blue,
          Hair slaked with lime,
            Sword and shield in hand,
              The thunder of hoof beats,
                Voices screaming curses at the foe!

Sing me a song in Gaelic,
    Of the good and the bad,
      The righteous and wicked,
        Of promises kept and broken,
          Bonds and betrayal,

Victories and losses!
Of the body and the spirit,
Life, death, and beyond!

Sing me a song in Gaelic
So I may know who I am,
Strong and proud,
Melancholic and mournful,
Aware of the blood-stained ground I daily trod.

Let my courage soar,
Even if buoyed by mead,
Let my eyes rise,
And become one with the spiraling smoke.

Sing me song in Gaelic,
Of a misty dawns,
Stone-filled lands,
Lavender fields of heather and moss,
Grass greener than green,
Hay more golden than gold!
A horse alive, eager to be greeted,
Whinnying, ready for the fray!

Sing me a song in Gaelic . . .
That speaks of a quiet-watered land . . . .
Then sing it again to the world.

A DRINKER'S HAMLET 1

Hamlet (Act 3, Scene 1) William Shakespeare (Marsella 1975 - Revision and Update)

To drink, or not to drink,
That is the question:

Whether tis nobler in the mind to suffer
The slings and arrows of outrageous fortune,
Or to take refuge from the sea of troubles
With cup in hand, and by drinking deeply
Of the vines' ripe fruit, end them.

Ah, to drink, and with our sips
To end the heartaches and the thousand natural shocks
Flesh is heir to;
Nay, to refrain, and with the virtue
Therein derived,
Face the onslaught, full strength alone.
Aye, that's the rub!

To drink or not to drink!
Do we deceive ourself
To speak of drink as food, balm, or social oil?

Is no virtue to be found in bottle's refuge?
Should our backs bear burdens,
Calumny's barbs, law's abuses,
Friends' betrayals, love's losses,

Penury's pains?
Conscience doth make cowards of us all!

What should such fellows, as we, do?
Stand before the foe?
Bend beneath the load?
Weep aloud, wail in silence?
Mourn we are caught between heaven and earth.

Comment:

I do not drink, nor use illegal substances. I first wrote this revision of Hamlet's soliloquy in 1975 for a book chapter on alcoholism. I thought it would be interesting to apply Shakespeare's words and meter to the problem -- my apologies to William, and to Hamlet.

At one point in my internship years, when I was working as a clinical psychologist in a mental hospital in Massachusetts, I came upon a patient assigned to the woodshop drinking turpentine from a small white and green metal can. I was shocked. I could not believe what I was seeing?

No amount of reading could have taught me more than that one moment, the sheer power alcohol commands over an addicted person. I remembered the plaintive look in his eyes as he saw me: "Could I understand his plight? What could he do? Caught, as he was, between heaven and earth?"

Sisters: Anguish in Time and Place
(Fiction Story)

Legacy of Sisterhood . . .

Alice sighed! There was much behind her sigh: regret, grief, resignation, the story of her life. It was a melancholic sigh, each exhaled breath hovering above her -- misty clouds adding to each day's difficulties, limiting understanding, hiding any chance for relief. And now this! Yet another closing point for her life, another sorrow.

Beth would need constant care. Beth was in her final days. A rest home close to their older brother, Andrew, would be a better place for her. It was time for goodbyes.

In their youth together on the farm, Alice envied Beth. Beth was always so strong. She seemed to know just what to say and what do in any situation, especially around the dinner table, when the family was gathered: Father, mother, older brother, Andrew, Beth, and Alice. Proper behavior was expected, but Beth always seemed to add her distinct style to the "proper" behavior.

Alice missed Beth when Beth left the farm for college to study special education and student counseling. She brought college books home, and Alice poured through them in awe at their contents. Unlike Beth, Alice stopped attending Ashford College after a semester. Events made it impossible for her to return, to recover from painful experiences. The sisters took different paths.

Beth left the farm, moved to a city, and became a respected and revered counselor of children with special needs. She loved her work!

Her mind was alert and interested in the world about her. She had a quiet presence, but she would not be denied.

Alice loved it when Beth would speak with Alice's husband, Frederick, quietly educating him on what was occurring in the world beyond the farm. She would say: "Frederick, this is a war of ideologies, ways of life. Some people believe this farm should be owned by the government."

Frederick would smile, turn away, and say: "There is no way this farm is going to be owned by anyone else than me and Alice. This is my land!"

After leaving Ashford College, Alice remained on the farm in Willow, Indiana. She was a farm child, a farm daughter, and eventually, she would become a farm wife and farm mother. No escape! Alice took a job as a clerk in a bakery shop in town. She met Frederick in the bakery shop. He stopped by daily for pastries on is way to work at the foundry. Alice found Frederick charming, although she was uncomfortable with his bold confidence and self-assurance.

"I believe I'll have three of those! Do you think I should take four?" Fred would say to promote conversation in the bakery. He enjoyed throwing Alice off kilter. He was flirting! She did not know anything witty to say in return. Finally, she said: "Four is my favorite number! But don't ask me why! It just is! (Take that Mr. Flirt!). If you want four, I will pack four for you. How many do you want?"

Both smiled! She had met his self assurance with wit and charm, and she was proud of herself. Fred would look at her, enjoying her discomfort and effort after being assertive, knowing she enjoyed the interchange. Yet he was never willing to yield his obvious control of the situation. Finally, to make the situation work to his advantage, Fred said: "I'll take five of those then! Want to have some extra for the mill." Alice nodded and smiled in complete surrender. Frederick made her laugh!

In some ways, marriage was inevitable. Alice knew her parents wanted to move from the farm and be closer to town. They would either have to to sell the farm, or one of the children would have to take it over. There was a problem: Walter wanted to be a minister; Beth wanted to live in a big city; and this left, Alice. With the right husband, the farm could be kept in the family.

Frederick knew farming, and he knew Alice's family's farm was a choice property, capable of expansion. He thought to himself: "That farm could raise wheat, corn, and soy beans, and there was room for raising beef." He could do what was necessary to make it profitable. He knew he could make the farm a home for Alice and for coming children.

Alice felt secure with Frederick. He was strong! He commanded presence. She thought her mother and father, even with their reserve, would like him. There were few other opportunities for her to meet men in her life. The bakery shop customers were mainly women, buying treats for their family. Living on an isolated country farm offered few chances for love! Alice looked at her dresser mirror. She was not a beauty! Glasses, no makeup, simple hair style and clothes! But she thought she would make a good wife and mother. There was comfort in the familiar.

Enter Frederick . . .

For Frederick, marriage to Alice was a financial and personal windfall. Within years, he would escape the poverty of his own early life on a farm in Indiana, and come to co-own Alice's family farm. The farm was ideally located, distant enough for privacy and seclusion, but close enough to town for work and needed purchases.

Frederick wasn't educated above high school, but he knew farming! He watched his father farm the land they owned, and he learned the demands of animals, grains, and equipment. He yearned to own his own farm one day, if only to show his parents and brothers and sisters, his many skills and abilities. Amid the somberness of his youth in a poor rural family, any pursuit of being different, especially better, was discouraged by stares and glares. By eighteen, he helped on the farm, and worked nights in the town. He was determined to move away from his family.

Frederick's flat feet kept him from serving in WWII. This gave him a chance to rise as a foreman in the local iron forge tool factory -- now an essential war-industry product. His future possibilities for wealth and position were increasing. The war years were years in which Frederick thrived personally and financially, securing his life as a foreman, and as a farmer.

Alice and Frederick married before the outbreak of World War II. The world was on edge, but in Willow, Indiana, routines were pursed without change. Alice's elderly parents moved to a small house in town. The farm was turned over to Alice and Frederick for a small deeded loan. It was a beginning. Alice became a farmer's wife, skilled in rural-life requirements: cooking, washing clothes, baking pies, canning foods, eventually raising ten children, and all the time, caring for elderly parents in town. In time, she came to understand her own anxieties would keep her captive to this place for all her life.

Anguish . . .

Alice's sigh affirmed her unspoken pain, her endless stream of heartaches, disappointment, and grief. She had so hoped her ageing years, free now from the burdens of farm life, raising ten children, and efforts to please a demanding autocratic husband, would bring her relief and comfort. She sought a time when a welcoming calm would descend upon her, and her prayers would bring her inner peace.

Alice recalled a word she had once read in a Billy Graham prayer book – *equanimity.* She had looked up its meaning in the dictionary, read the words, and felt it captured much of what she was seeking -- calmness, inner peace, balance, and composure -- all needed to meet the endless daily demands of a farm wife and farm mother of nine children.

The demands never stopped. One demand would be followed by another. The voices echoed in her ears: "Don't forget to boil the jars for canning; the beans are ready for picking!" "Mom, I don't want jam on my sandwich." "Alice, I am going to bring some help out for harvesting. We will need lunch for six inside for a week." "Will you drive me to the church dance on Friday?" "Mom, do I have a clean shirt for school?"

Now, again, life would require more suffering, more bearing up, more surrender of self to punitive tolls. Alice wondered to herself: "Does it ever end? Is there ever a point when I will be free of suffering . . . sorrow?"

Alice recalled Beth had once used the word "anguish" in response to Alice's sharing her feelings. "I am sorry, Alice," Beth said. "You have had so much anguish in your life." Helen nodded in agreement at the time. The word "anguish" reverberated in her mind. She had never forgotten Beth's observation, and choice of word. It so summed up her life: "Anguish ... anguish! Yes, anguish, never-ending anguish!" The very sound of the word captured everything she felt.

Now it was time to add yet another sorrow to her chain of memories. Her life was repeating itself again and again. The same endless cycle of caring for others, comforting them, consoling them, even as she herself needed support and nurturing.

"Why has this fate befallen me?" Alice thought.

"Why? Dear God, I have no more to give. Forgive me." Alice felt guilty by her complaint.

"The Lord is my shepherd, I shall not want." Alice recited the words of the 23rd Psalm to herself, trying to calm her disappointment. She had recited the words so many times in her life, always drawing comfort from the simple belief the Lord was always with her. She should not ask for more. The Lord would help.

Alice placed her thoughts aside, and stared at Beth sitting in the old stuffed chair. She tried to fix the image in her mind even as it brought her agony: a single lamp lit a darkened room, a small table with some prescription plastic pill vials, a half-filled glass of water, a ticking clock, and her forlorn and dying sister sitting in her favorite chair, the only furniture item she brought with her when she moved from trailer-park home in Indiana.

Beth was alert to the moment, and smiled gently at Alice. Her blue eyes twinkled, enhanced by tears. "I'm going to be alright, Alice. Don't be worrying about me. I know how to manage, and with care-home help, I will be comfortable. Old age takes away control. I am not what I used to be. But I saw it coming!" Beth said with a knowing smile.

Beth had lived alone for 45 years, following her divorce from an alcoholic husband. She had been warned by her parents: "This is not the right man for you or our family." He owned a bar! That itself was cause for concern. Like Alice, Beth had known sorrows, but she chose withdrawal and isolation when the divorce came.

She did not need to hear the litany of "We told you so, Beth! You never would listen to us." Most of all she hated the silent and unrelenting stares! Words were sparse, but communication was complete, and could be devastating! She thought to herself: "Silence can kill as easy as words."

Beth's only child, Tim, had a drinking problem like his father. Beth always said: "We don't give enough credit to genetics! We inherit more than we know." And then she would pause, smile, and ask rhetorically to those present: "I wonder what I inherited from my father and my mother, and all those who came before them – Jefferson's and Fosters? Cold English reserve! Don't complain!"

Beth was formal and detailed in her speech. There were no wasted words. She modeled politeness and civility, but she also was direct in her answers and comment. Her directness created the social distance she preferred. She had also come to learn that it gave her an obvious air of imperturbability. She was in control. She liked being above the fray: present, but aloof; a careful observer and a commentator – "An interpreter of life," according to Beth.

Beth knew her style added to her life's problems. Tim remained distant from her, living in Pittsburgh, following a divorce from his beautiful wife, Barbara. They had four daughters. Beth took great pride in her grandchildren. She would share their photos: "Aren't they cute? I think they have Tim's eyes. Genetics!" She did not leave room for disagreement with her unspoken conclusion. Tim had inherited her watery-blue eyes!

"Should I call the children?" Alice asked mournfully.

Beth thought for a few moments: "I think it is best they not see me looking like this? I saw them a few years ago, when I looked better. Let them remember me from that time."

Beth overtly accepted her plight with quiet dignity, but her help-lessness was a constant inner source of distress. She did not like having to depend on others, even as she knew it was inevitable. In a few hours, her paid caretaker would come to bathe and clean her. It was insufferable -- a violation of her privacy -- her separateness, touching, soaping, rubbing, staring.

Beth knew her behavior could be a problem. It was why she came to live alone. That was the way she was! She would never be a gregarious outgoing person. She would remain reserved and composed, never losing control, using smiles, soft touches, and patience in her 45 year counseling and teaching career with disabled children. In the end she endured the silences, the absence of others in the night -- finding solace in reading books, especially reading the Bible.

"What else can I do given the circumstances," she wondered to herself? She had an accurate view of her life, and its limited possibilities. She would say to herself: "Look I am obese, white-haired, be-spectacled, unattractive, and introverted. In addition, I am opinionated! Why would anyone want me as a companion?" And then she would smile to herself, and say: "I will be my own companion. No problems that way."

Beth grasped the worn and aged Bible, on her lap, a Bible given to her in youth by her mother and father. It was now more than 80 years old, its cover and pages bent and worn, much as Beth. She recalled a brief conversation with her Bible one evening as she clutched it in her hands. The memories flowed.

"Well, Bible! Time for another meeting! You have been with me for so many years, offering your wisdom. I am grateful. Thank you! You keep me from crying. I don't want to cry. Maybe I should cry. I remember reading verses on crying." Beth tuned the Bible's pages. She had flagged Luke, 7:13. She recited: "And when the Lord saw her, he had compassion on her, and said to her, 'Do not weep.' Beth placed the Bible on her lap. She had read verses seeking comfort, and salvation. "It was time now," she thought."

Beth was 82, and disabled by growing symptoms of Parkinson's disease. Even her voice quivered. Her mind was still alert, and she could speak clearly but with a shaking and tremulous voice.

Alice had asked Frederick if Beth could stay with them, at least for awhile, until Alice was no longer able to care for Beth. But now disorders were moving forward on both sides. Beth's mind was still clear, even as her body began to fail. An upstairs bedroom was not the right place. It was too much for Alice to walk up the ten stairs, bringing coffee, food, or good company, as she watched Beth's growing problems.

Both Alice and Beth were overweight, and movement had never been easy for either. Their shoulders were rounded, backs arched and bent from sagging breasts; hips were large, stomachs protruded, legs

226

were heavy with veins, and knees were swollen. They knew the images they presented.

In their own minds, however, they saw each other as beautiful, ignoring bodies in favor of presence and shared life. Each understood the other, and the tolls life had taken from the time of their childhood. They affirmed and comforted each other's life.

Two Sisters . . .

The two sisters stared at each other trying to come to some understanding of the situation -- an understanding of their lives, how they unfolded and passed so quickly. There was a now a brief time for amends, for taking up the loose ends that had accumulated. What could they make of it all? They sat in silence looking at one another with tears in their eyes. Each searched for words. It was an unfolding of years of images and memories -- a culmination – a coming together of people, events, feelings forged for years, now too late to undo.

Each knew their fate, and each knew there was little comfort beyond the quiet stares and words they offered each other. Some words would help – prayer, humor, love, shared memories of years together and apart. The words would be a sealing of their lives!

She once told Alice, in wry humor: "A voice with no body."

Beth could no longer live alone, and she had accepted Alice's invitation to take a small upstairs bedroom in Alice's house; but the disease progressed more rapidly than expected. Alice, the younger sister at 77, was trying to help, as she always had, but signs of her own problems had become noticeable to her. She kept these problems to herself, and did not share them with her husband, Frederick, or the children. She was forgetting simple things!

Increasingly, Alice had begun to wonder if Frederick was noticing: "Forgetting names of friends . . . playing the right cards in pinochle . . . small mistakes in cooking . . . and even remembering to flush the toilet."

She knew something was wrong, but she kept saying it was a result of too many worries on her mind. She would think something, and then forget it. "Why did I go in this room?" Where did I place my keys? Why did I leave them on the stove?"

Beth noticed her own breathing was labored. A rare home visit by a physician revealed her heart was failing. Too much weight, too little movement, it was only a matter of time. "Too little time," she thought. "Where did the time go? I let it pass each day, never understanding one day it would all be gone."

Beth refused to yield to the gloomy thoughts: "So this is what it all comes to in the end. This is what it all adds up to after years of denial. Now I am expected to believe in heaven, and to have faith, so I can get to heaven, some way or the other."

Beth's doubts made her uncomfortable, even as she entertained them, but she would not compromise her style, even in final days. She loved being the curmudgeon, even with God. It was a way for her to question, to learn, and to satisfy her own curiosities about life.

Her older brother, Andrew, had chosen the ministry, and he never seemed to have any doubts or questions that could not be answered by Biblical references. "The Lord giveth, and the Lord taketh away. Blessed be the name of the Lord." And he would start to hum and sing, "Oh Lord, my God . . . . ""Join me, Beth!" Beth would smile, but not sing.

Beth, as the middle-child, had rebelled against the certainties and absolutes of life of her upbringing on Midwestern Gothic farm. She found it hard to conform to the culture of constant reminders – do not stray from God, work hard, and contain temptations. If she strayed from the expected paths, her parents would remind her of the proper way -- shaming her at the dinner table in front of her older brother, Andrew. Andrew would nod in agreement, already on the path to becoming a Christian minister.

What troubled her more was their shaming her in front of her younger sister, Alice. Beth would sit silently, even as she wanted to say respectfully: "Father, mother, Andrew, there are many paths to heaven." Alice sat quietly, swallowing the words, as she ate the food before her. When no one was watching, Alice would smile at Beth. It was their shared joke!

But Alice was confused! She loved Beth. Was Beth a source of vice as her parents implied? Alice remembered the Dickinson poem, "The world is too much with us." Beth was the world, in the eyes of her parents and brother, Andrew! The world! A place outside the farm: "Did it exist?"

Beth's intelligence made it more difficult for herself and everyone in the family. She was always filled with questions about things. The family discouraged her from learning things beyond the farm. The very impulses she had for questioning everything – an unsatisfied inquiry -- had come to make her uncomfortable and withdrawn from people. "What am I supposed to do? Just be quiet and smile?"

Under constant stares and words from her parents, Beth began to feel uncomfortable with herself and her parents. Beth wondered when she was young whether she should go to Paris in the 1930s. It seemed so exotic and appealing -- the writers, artists, freedom. She even picked up some French phrases just in case. They could always be used with friends who were amazed at her quiet, but undeniable presence. *"Je nais se pas, mon Ami! C'est un gran problem, pour le monde – et aussi pour moi!"*

Beth's thoughts brought her comfort and discomfort. She had been raised to accept Christian beliefs without question. Yet the years of being alone in her trailer had left her with many unanswered questions. She went to church on Sunday! Prayed in silence, she sang the hymns, listened to the sermons. Every now and then, there was a good one – one that seemed reasonable to her educated mind; one permitting individual opinion. She used the term, "Selective acceptance of Bible truths." Now it was decision time: "To believe, or not to believe!" She grasped the Bible.

She knew the comforts of complete belief, but she could not accept self-deception: "Life after death? Maybe! Heaven - Hell? Who knows?" She conjured up the image of skipping around on clouds with bearded men, angels, harps. "Sounds boring," she muttered sarcastically. "But maybe they will leave me alone -- just as long as it is not Detroit!"

"Thank you, Alice! You have always been a wonderful little sister," Beth said slowly with her tremulous voice.

Beth had always spoken with a clipped-word style of speech. Each word she said seemed to exist on its own, and one had to listen for the entire sentence to get what she was saying. She had noticed that others were aware of her speech, and she would often say in response: "I taught and counseled children with disabilities for almost 50 years. You have to speak slowly and clearly, so they understand."

But there was something prescient years ago in her clear but tremulous speaking, signaling the eventual onset of Parkinson's disease. Beth wondered: "Was it the years of growing up on the farm, inhaling the chemicals cast on the ground? Was there something in the terrible tasting well-water and collected rain water washing off an aluminum roof? Was there something in the trailer? Paints and stains contain formaldehyde. Or was it inherited? Or was it both?"

"We should have spent more time together, Beth," Alice said. "We are sisters! Isn't that what sisters are supposed to do?" Alice lamented. "I mean, why did we let all the time pass without being with one another more often than a holiday?" Alice nodded her head to express her disappointment with their missed past.

"God knows I needed you so often, Beth, I needed someone who could understand. Someone who would understand what I was going through each day was difficult, exhausting, and someone who would encourage me to bear up under the burdens, and to keep going."

"I had no one, Beth! And Fred was no help later! He was just as cold as his mother! Never did like his family!"

Alice continued speaking: "I didn't want to bother you, but now I wish I would have because it would have brought us closer together." Alice felt guilty speaking of herself at a time when Beth had her own problems. "I'm sorry, Beth," Alice said apologetically.

"Don't be sorry, Alice! You are right! Why does it take a lifetime to know what we should have done; and then when we finally know, it is too late to correct it?"

Alice smiled at Beth's typical insights and wisdom. Beth continued speaking, wanting both of them to better understand their situation.

"It seems to me we really did not have much choice given the way we were reared -- the farm, Mother and Father, religion." She paused and thought about her next words.

"It just kept us from one another. It was almost as if we were not supposed to enter each other's lives. We were supposed to go our ways. And we did! We cared for one another, in our own distant ways, but we were not supposed to interfere. We were supposed to give one another space. In the end, that is not a good thing for a family. We loved one another, but we forgot love. We were family, with no love ties."

Beth was shocked at her own words. The words acknowledged disappointment, and more than that, resentment. It was as if the revelation sealed their lives. Beth did not want to hurt Alice, nor suggest Alice was to blame for the conclusion she had reached. She looked at Alice, and added words she thought would soften her conclusion.

"Alice, some times "It was almost as if God had planned our fates, and we were supposed to follow. Like it was all pre-ordained!" Beth paused, aware her breathing was more difficult as a result of her distress.

"I know you wanted more from me when we were growing up, Alice, but I think Mother thought I might interfere with her teachings. And she was probably right. I would have given you more questions than answers. We were too distant from each other. Everything was fixed. Darned those Calvinists! I thought Wesley had solved the problem when he said our God is a loving God."

Beth grinned at her audacity. She was amused with her accusation.

"Don't tell, Andrew I said that. He will have to give me an answer, and I don't need some Bible story that has nothing to do with the Puritans, and what they left behind for us. All I know is I wanted to go to Paris, and I didn't want to feel guilty about going!" I just wanted freedom, space to be myself! No room for that in our family! Just fit in!"

"We never hugged much, Alice," Beth said as tears welled in her eyes. "I wanted to hug you all the time, but Mother would have frowned on that. Too excessive! Unnecessary! Embarrassing!"

Alice looked at Beth pensively, deeply, wanting to hold her and never let go.

"I wish you would have hugged me, Beth. I wanted to be hugged! I wanted you to hug me. I was so naïve about life. All I knew was the farm and Willow High School. I was so afraid so often. It was as if I didn't fit in anywhere. I just wanted some consoling, some assurance that things would work out. I kept reciting the 23rd Psalm all the time. I began to think people would hear me speaking to myself. A hug would have helped me so much!"

"And do you recall how few compliments we got!" Alice said. "It was almost as if we were supposed or expected to do what we did without any praise. It was just the right thing! We never had much fun! Well I never had much fun! Fun for me was eating an apple pie, or baking one.

232

Alice continued: "I liked holiday times. Fun was permitted! But even then, there was no praise or thank you! There were so few compliments! And the compliments were always indirect, like when father would say about my pie: *"That's a blue ribbon pie at the Grange."* Why not say something more personal! Something like, you are a great cook, and I am proud of you, and I love you."

"I agree, Alice," Beth said with resignation.

"I think we never bonded as a family. We were people living together, but we were always apart. And now it is too late! But at least now we recognize what we should have done and been. We were all so uncomfortable with emotion. There were times I wanted to just dance across that living room floor, throwing my hands in the air, and even wiggling my hips. But that was unacceptable. Can't you hear father saying: "Christian women don't do that!" And mother would interject, "Beth, come help me and Alice in the kitchen with this pie."

"I was so torn," Beth continued, more confident now in her thoughts; more willing to acknowledge regret, even at this late point in her life.

"I wanted to escape the farm and the farm way-of-life. Remember all those Sunday sermons telling us how we were born with evil, and needed to repent. How we were sinners? Where did they come up with that one? Andrew loved Cotton Mather. I did not!"

Once I looked at myself standing nude before the mirror," Beth continued, "And I was worried lightning from the sky would strike me for doing so. It made me live my life in constant fear and anger, and I refused to do so."

"I believe in God, Alice, but I no longer believe he -- or she -- wants to punish us. That's Calvin's mistake," Beth said owning her blasphemy.

"Wesley was right! God is love! God is finding love within us and loving others. All the rest is just . . . "Beth paused, seeking an answer to her assertion . . . "Cotton Mather! Old depressed men in black capes taking out their own despair and anger on the world!"

Alice placed her hand over her mouth and laughed. Beth chuckled at her own reply. "Depressed men! Yes, that's the answer." Seconds passed. Beth assumed a more serious look on her face.

"But we just could not escape the old ways. Alice. Restraint was expected. No displays of emotion. Father was so strong! If you disagreed with him, he would point to the door! I think Mother was more sensitive to us. But she too feared Father's anger!"

Alice smiled at her sister's words! She loved Beth's defiance. Beth was this magical farm-bred, Christian-raised, self-shaped contrarian who refused to be suppressed. She was never a penitent!

Alice wiped a tear from her cheek. She rose, went over to Beth, and hugged her deeply. A healing hug – a hug shared by those who struggled together and were finally willing to speak truth. Each was aware of the importance of this moment in their lives.

They had regrets, but it was too late to change. They had been absent in each others' lives. They had not helped one another, even as they knew help was wanted. It was not the way they had been taught! This was not to be the way to be! There was an unspoken and omnipresent style of life for mid-western rural Gothic life! It was ingrained in their parents, and perhaps in their genes.

Their fate was sealed by times and places. Alice and Beth were pushed by their past toward fixed roles, denying them an opportunity to escape, to explore, to find fulfillment of their unique talents and potential. Their intelligence was obvious. But personal circumstances kept them prisoner. Their minds and lives would always be captive to the anguish of place and time, even as their hearts yearned for more.

Beth looked at Alice: "It is okay to yearn! It is worst to regret."

As I Age . . .

Thoughts on Memory and Cosmos

"For of all sad words of tongue or pen,
The saddest are these:
'It might have been!'"

John Greenleaf Whittier (1807–1892)

"If only. . . ."

Weeks ago, I spoke with a friend of many years. Typically, we remain in close contact, exchanging emails and phone calls on a regular basis. However, I noticed he had stopped our contacts. My efforts to reach him went unanswered. Finally, I phoned and spoke with his wife. I asked how he was; I told her I missed him. She said he had not been well. She stated he seemed "depressed."

Later, prompted by his wife, he phoned me, and, as she had said, he told me he had been feeling "depressed." He added as he approached 80 years of age, he was filled with thoughts of regret and his inevitable passing. "There were," he said, "so many things I wish I would have done; so many things I wish I would not have done." *"For of all sad words of tongue or pen. . . ."*

"Aye, there's the rub," Shakespeare wrote! I suspect all ageing people feel this way. There is an inclination as we age to recall and relive *"If only . . ."* memories. This is, in many ways, an effort to make sense of events in our lives — what we perceive occurred and has

not occurred. I once wrote some brief lines: *"If: A two-letter word, simple in sound, profound in consequence."*

The reality is the omnipresence of memories, as we recall them, as we wish to recall them, and as we wish to forget them. Memories are always present, waiting to be released. And with each memory comes an endless flow of associations. Memories work their way to the surface, the immediacy of the present moment. They are sources of joy, sources of grief, sources of insight, and sources of regret and resentment. They are also sources shaping our future, sources for understanding who we are becoming.

As I age, I find my thoughts returning to the days of my youth, to accumulated memories of people, places, and events once stored unobtrusively in my brain, now awaiting chances to be revived, to be considered, and to order my life, to fuse past, present, and future.

I believe preoccupation with my past is not a chance event. Rather, I think ageing is compelling me to examine who I am today by ordering my past in an endless process of recall, reconsideration, recovery, and reevaluation. The process of recalling and ordering past, present, and future is bewildering and exhilarating; it is also exhausting.

Memories flow into one another with a rhyme and reason known to their sources, often oblivious to my efforts to assign order to their existence. The memories have connections I never imagined. I search for the "mystery" of their attachments and associations, the possibilities, even as I remain hesitant to accept linkages across time and place.

In my search, I recognize there is a need for "abductive" reasoning. There may be a necessary chain of cause and association, but this does not mean the cause and association are sufficient. Care is needed in the journey to unlock mind. Ahhh, the pleasures and demons of inquiry!

I begin with recalling an image of a person's face from my past, but soon I am flooded with chains of associations distant in time, place, and consequence, relevant, it seems to me, to the very moment of my initial recall. Time is compressed, time is repressed, time unfolds, and time is transcended.

The free association methods of psychoanalysis, proposed by Sigmund Freud and others, are a therapeutic method for exploring an analysand's past. Of course, the cost is far less if you do it yourself, although care must be taken as the natural inclinations to repress, deny, and deceive must be mediated.

As I reflect on my memories, I wonder if I am engaging in a natural and essential evolutionary process, a process driven by impulses to make sense, to make meaning of the life's unfolding flow. Birth, life, death! A straightforward flow! But along the way, of course, there are inordinate experiences accumulating, exacting tolls, and offering opportunities for discovering and fixing identity and for making meaning of existence. Hmm?

This memory inquiry process in ageing is challenging, filled with discomforts and regrets. I cannot change nor reverse so much of what has occurred. How do you teach youth, still unfettered with regrets, to make good choices? Can they ever grasp that one day they or others will open an account ledger. *"Oh my God, did I say that? Did I do that? What was I thinking of at the time? I am shocked as I hear my words."*

What of permanent memories? What of permanent regrets? Am I to remain captive? If acts I regret are of such violation and destruction, then repentance challenges my mind, body, and spirit. This is the tragedy of war: the permanence of traumatic memories resisting forgiveness, festering, begging for release from an imprint, a deep engram never to be erased. For the person without conscience, memories may be of no consequence. Here the only issue is whether conscience can be born, recovered, or renewed. But for most of humanity, the issue of negotiating regrets is omnipresent.

Memories — Then and Now

Now, as I enter the autumn of my years, I am drawn to the process of recall and response each day. I understand the value of focusing on the moment, but my memories refuse to be denied, entering and coloring my life each moment, regardless of the daily tasks before me. More and more I recognize the entry of memories is not an intrusion, but it is rather a process enriching my life by inviting me to give context to who I am at this point in my ageing life. Is the very awareness of my future, the inevitable, encouraging me to reflect, to make sense, if possible, of inevitable mortality amidst awareness of consciousness, choice, and moral virtue.

Initially, I was perplexed by the constant return of memories, each memory demanding reconsideration at "unexpected" moments, seeking a new place, position, and importance in my being, a reconstruction of being, a renewal, but not necessarily one of comfort and gratification. I concluded there was an "effort after meaning," an effort to make sense of purpose–identity–causality connections. Who am I? Who have I been? Who am I becoming? The process compels me to ask again and again basic existential questions, finding contentment only to become disquieted a cycle.

I ask myself whether my identity should now stable and stronger no longer subject to the doubts, uncertainties, and angst of adolescent years. Perhaps, however, it is better to grasp that purpose and identity are lifelong quests. Purpose and identity are not limited to certain ages or stages.

I am pressed, pushed, and pulled to reflect on myself in a continuing effort after purpose and identity and, with hope with them will come a related sense of "fulfillment" or "satisfaction," and finally, the opportunity to seek answers, pose questions, and doubt, endlessly. Ahhh, the beauty of biased reasoning and thought.

The Nuances and Consequences of Convention

Perhaps memory intrusions are reminders to pursue reconciliation of past and present, to negotiate fact and fiction, to grasp the merging of reality and fantasy, and to better understand being and becoming all at a precise, important moment, a convergence of identity, time, and place. Much of this process, as I wrote at the beginning of this commentary, involves the word **"If."**

"If only" . . . "if only" . . . the desire to erase past regrets is endless, but the reality of their existence is not, they are there, and they can only be negotiated by acceptance, forgiveness, or invoking some rationalization that dulls their presence. Unless it is truly an unforgivable event or occurrence, we are offered an opportunity to place it in our present context. There is something wonderful about ageing that enables an understanding of why things were done.

I am fond of the phrase, popular at this moment: *"Life is difficult for everyone! Be kind!"* We are caught in an ocean of laws, rules, retributions, regulations, morals, commandments, admonishments, and expectations. *"Conscience does make cowards of us all,"* wrote William Shakespeare in the 16th century.

Sigmund Freud understood conscience in the same way when he wrote his brilliant volume, *Civilization and its Discontents,* in the early 20th century. He did so as unrelenting Victorian morals of the day imposed repressions upon natural urges and impulses. Freud captured the dilemma of life in his tripartite personality structure — Id, Ego, Superego. We know, of course, there is a gap between articulated morals and reality. Life in society requires acceptance and conformity to the norms and convention. Violate them, and there are consequences! Sometimes, the harshest consequences come from within our own mind, conscience (i.e., superego), as reveries of the past bring forth a tide of things we wish we would not have said or done.

It took me years to grasp how harsh society's dictums and proprieties can be upon the human mind, demanding more than we are capable of following. Guilt, shame, self-blame, and condemnation occur reflexively. We fall before the dictums and proprieties recalled as we age. Amid tired and weary minds, we seek forgiveness and ask release from a harsh penance.

I had to learn the wisdom of selective detachment! I also had to learn there are selective ways to critique and evaluate society, not only for my preferences, but also to encourage others to explore their lives amidst society's accepted conventions.

Pursuing Reconciliation

I am not a man caught in depression, despair, or melancholy. Indeed, quite the opposite. I find myself, at this very moment in time, more alert and conscious of the complexities of life: personal life, collective life, and natural life. I am aware more than at any prior time in my life. History is our story! History is my story! It can be read and understood, if one chooses, as the narrative of a species "pushed" and "pulled" by forces inherent in human evolution and in cosmic creation. That is the mystery!

Life unfolds before us! Choices are made! How little prepared we are for the delicate balancing act we face each day. Life can be read and understood as the narrative of an individual mind and body caught in the flow of life, conscious of choice but limited by frailties and strengths of the moment. Choices are a function of freedom! Freedom, too often, is a function of roles and statuses: men have more choices than women; the rich have more choices than the poor; educated people have more choices than uneducated people, and whites have more choices than people of color!

In the present moments of my existence, I probe my mind, recalling events and people from my past, an array of images and feelings, vague and clear, clouded and transparent, misty and vibrant, all documenting my life! The accumulation is my story! I try to attach meaning, to cast my memories within a rationale appropriate to their time and also to this moment.

It is an effort after meaning. It is making meaning. It is a process which seals time and experiences, rendering judgment and evaluation. How much can I deny? How much can I change? How much can I accept? Life is difficult! "Forgive and forget" or "try to forget, and try to forgive" or "forgive and remember" or "whatever. . ."? Memories! They are the key!

Some Closing Thoughts

What can I say? I say we should consider life a privilege. It is better to be alive, to have experienced life, even with its trials and tribulations.

Groucho Marx, the sagacious comedian, one said, *"Do you think life is hard? Try the opposite!"* Some people do, and, at some point, we all do! We are, as human beings, unique, a one-time miracle, accumulating experience, learning, changing, adjusting, and adapting.

We are capable of regretting and yet renewing by forgiving ourselves and others. The word **"if,"** as I wrote at the beginning of this commentary, has the power to bring much regret into our lives. But regret can also be an opportunity to forgive oneself, to forgive others and, in doing so, to grasp life is about renewal and resurrection each day.

Life, it seems to me, is about pursuing understanding of the larger order of things and positioning ourselves in this timeless flow beginning not just with our conception and birth, but also with the very moment our universe was "born"! In a time beyond our comprehension, from a compressed energy–matter particle came an explosion still echoing across time and space, still part of this unfolding of life as fission and fusion.

We are gifted with life, not as a chance event, but as a part of a larger unfolding or evolution of the cosmos itself. We are part of the very force that animates the universe. On a star-filled evening on the shores of the Pacific Ocean, I gazed at the heavens. I was lost in their endlessness — their infinity. But . . . I was aware and attentive to the experience! I beheld the glory, conscious of the grandeur and the splendor. I was filled with awe and reverence as I grasped the wonder, even as I was aware I was but a speck amidst infinity! I was a "conscious" speck!

In that moment, the cosmic complexity of life was revealed to me, the connection among all things! The "order" and "chaos" were unfolding mysteries beyond my comprehension but not my awareness. Amidst my limited knowledge, I imagined an unfolding cosmic equation descending and ascending in a whirling moment upon and from me.

Cosmic creation, fission and fusion, separation and connection, diversity and unity, consciousness and choice, morality and virtue, belief and doubt, being and becoming, life/death, transcendence. . . .

From an infinitely compressed particle of matter and energy, a particle of unknown origin created itself in a cauldron of forces/matter exceeding comprehension, exploded with a force of infinite power of matter/energy into endless forms, patterns and existences, capable of substituting, interchanging, and interacting with each other in a cosmic dance amidst shifting masks. One cosmic moment: mass, one cosmic moment: energy! Visible/invisible! All of this an endless process unfolding toward . . . ?

Can I know? Should I know? Does GOD know? I recall the words from the creation hymn of the timeless *Rgveda*:

Not non-existent was it nor existent was it at that time; there was not atmosphere nor the heavens which are beyond. What existed? Where? In whose care? Water was it? An abyss unfathomable?

. . . .

Who, after all, knows? Who here will declare from whence it arose, whence this world? Subsequent are the gods to the creation of this world. Who then, knows when it came into being?

This world — whence it came into being, whether it was made or whether not —
He who is its overseer in the highest heavens, surely knows — or perhaps He knows not.

Creation Hymn: X. 129
Selections from the Rgveda
(In Maurer, 1986, p. 285)

In that precious moment I stood alone on a star-filled evening, I was not alone! And now, in this moment, I know 1 am part and whole! Acceptance of part and whole means connection: connection among all things, connection between self and others, connection across time and place, connection with past present and future.

Regrets? Yes! But how can I dismiss the incomprehensible yet comprehensible understanding of fission and fusion in all moments, in all places, and in all times?

I imagine all matter and energy from the moment of creation: from the "God particle" Higgs boson discovery to the most massive matter and energy instances, caught, by intention and purpose, in "nano" moments of time, in constant and simultaneous interaction, each moment yielding a new equation, an unfolding equation, driven by the past and pulled by the future. I swim now in thoughts of disproportion eluding my understanding yet urging me to continue. Life and death are not separate mysteries. There is only mystery: life/death!

While we know not what may transpire in death, a release of energy, a transformation of energy, a continuation of consciousness, an ascent for the virtuous, we do know in our moments of existence, the birth–life–death cycle: There is an effort after meaning, an effort to make sense of it all, an inquiry into identity, meaning, and purpose. For this process to unfold, exploring **memories** in ageing, indeed, at all ages, enriches life. It adds depth, substance, and liberation.

It is this archetypal? Is this inherent in each of my cells? Is this inherent in all cells? Is this it a cosmic code, a union of unfolding life/death in a continual existence? Is this what we call GOD? Is this what we call incarnation? I don't know! I can live with that! I can die with that!

REFERENCES:

Marsella, A.J. (1999). In search of meaning: Some thoughts on belief, doubt, and well-being. *The International Journal of Transpersonal Studies, 18,* 41–52.

Marsella, A.J. (2013). As I Age. Posted: 09/09/2013 5:00 pm. *Huntington Post Hawaii.*

Mauer, W. (1986). *Pinnacles of India's past: Selections from the Rgveda.* Philadelphia, PA: John Benjamins Publishing.

244

The Days Pass Quickly Now...

I.

The days pass quickly now.
    I recall how long each day seemed in my youth.
        How I yearned to be an adult,
            Able to enjoy the freedoms of age!

Freedoms!
    Work, marriage, children, money, cars,
        Appliances, tools, furniture,
            Dishes, pots, pans!
                The accumulated debris of a lifetime,
                    Filling floors, shelves, corners, cabinets,
                    Minds!

Freedom indeed!
    How little I understood.
        If only someone would have taught me,
            Lessons that go untaught,
                Lessons learned from . . .

Would I have listened?
    Would I have understood?
        Would I have been grateful?

Each life is lived anew,
    Each experience inscribed.
        Indelible memories:
            Seconds of elation,

Moments of joy,
　　Days, months of pain, sorrow, regret.

II.

I yearn to share my past,
　　To tell what I have learned.
　　　Insights from habit, practice,
　　　　Wisdom from error,
　　　　　Good and bad.

I want to tell them to children and grandchildren.
　　No one wants to hear.
　　　With listening comes connection.
　　　　They seek escape!
　　　　　Freedom!

They fear what I have seen and done.
　　They heard the stories in their youth.
　　　Words from a father,
　　　　Lectures, stories, fables
　　　　　The same opening line,
　　　　　　"When I was young, I would . . . . ."

Fantasy:　　*"Tell me what I should know, Papa?*
　　　　　What should I expect?
　　　　　What should I do if . . . . . . ?
　　　　　How did you handle that, Papa?
　　　　　Tell me the story about Calcutta. . . . . Again!
　　　　　What do I regret. . . . . . ? "

They don't want to be reminded of what awaits.
　　They have already fashioned their lives,
　　　Distortions, defense lies.
　　　　They may share genes, blood, but . . . .

Your life is not their life.
　　They cannot do what you did,

Nor be what you were.
You cannot re-create your life in others.
Procreate, yes!
Re-create, no!

Leave them with their bliss,
You gave them life in a moment of passion.
You fulfilled your gender function . . . . .
A Pacific salmon struggling upstream to spawn ....

III.

I imagine family scenes,
Wife, children, dog — together,
Reveling in presence,
Content with talk,
Buoyed by connection!

Idyllic moments:
Pizza in bed,
Dog burrowing in blanket,
Laughing, tickling, teasing,
Joy present!

In the silence of dawn,
In the darkness of night,
I ask:
How did I make it through?
Doing what needed to be done!
Each day succeeding, failing, falling, rising,
An endless cycle!

No pawn of some grand design,
Content with being alive,
Driven by dreams,
No penitent on bended knee,
Begging, promising, renewing.

I brought to each day
>Whatever I had at the moment:
>>Energy, thought, desire,
>>>Anger, frustration, hope!

Day passed, night, another dawn.
>Marriage, children, work, money, health, weather,
>>The stuff of life:
>>>Luck, chance, coincidence, the unexpected,
>>>>Decisions, choices, options,
>>>>>Amidst uncertainty, doubt, fear, relief.

It is not despair I share.
>Only awareness,
>>Consciousness of time!
>>>There is no preparation for ageing:
>>>>Ailments, frailties, death,
>>>>>How little is taught.

Why should they listen?
>Why should they care?
>>The internet can answer any question.
>>And failing that, there are friends.

Why would children want to hear?
>To know what awaits them, denies possibilities.
>>"It will be different for me.
>>>I am not you."
>>>>I can see the look in their eyes.
>>>>>They say: "Do not invalidate my thinking."

Now at 70 (now 76), I awake!
>I make coffee in the pre-dawn.
>>I hear birds,
>>>See sky lighten.
>>>>Sit in silence,

Reflecting!
A lifetime compressed into seconds,
A tear . . . regret.

The minutes pass more slowly now.
Another shooting pain!
Agony!

Life is short.
Life is long.
Long enough to bring . . . .

Guidelines for Leading a Spiritual Life

A decade ago, I wrote some New Year resolutions to improve the quality of my life. The resolutions were a set of guidelines to make my life more spiritual, and less materialistic. I found them useful, and published them in a Honolulu newspaper as an op-ed article.

The resolutions received both praise and criticism. The criticism came from folks who considered my meanderings to contradict specific religious beliefs and teachings. Later, I shared the resolutions with a wider audience via various listservs and journal publications. Some readers wrote they posted the guidelines on their refrigerator door.

Today, I share the guidelines once again. I do so, because "spirituality" is an important arbiter of life satisfaction. While some dislike any "mystical" terms, most of us find connecting to larger forces beyond our material existence is valuable for several reasons: **First**, it speaks to the non-material aspects of our being as we are inundated with pressures to locate ourselves in our material world. **Second**, assigning "spirituality" a more prominent role and source of influence in our lives may promote a "social contagion," which can increase the importance of "connections" in all our lives. **Third**, leaving behind the material world in favor of connection to the larger cosmos and mysteries in which we live enables us to lose "ego," and to experience awe and reverence. How can these things be wrong or un-needed in a world in which so much is being done to destroy connections, and to empower the shadow side of human nature (e.g., war, violence, prejudice, hatred, selfishness)?

Growing Popularity of Spirituality

Any reading of the public, social, or private media today reveals an increased interest, concern and use – perhaps even pre-occupation – with the term "spirituality" and various related terms (e.g., spirit, spiritual, soul) embodying non-material states of existence. Initially, of course, the term spirituality was associated with various religious doctrines regarding ecclesiastical, clerical, and/or sacred experiences transcending secular life with the latter's material focus and priorities.

Spirituality has a special denotation and connotation which prizes a non-material essence or way-of-being in which it is assumed there is a perceived connection to events, forces, and beings that exist beyond the secular or temporal and physical world. The term "spirituality" often has been used to describe individuals whose existence and/or behavior transcended normal or conventional human concerns for meeting daily needs and demands, in favor of focus regarding broader human issues of meaning, purpose, social responsibility, and other higher-order priorities.

In my opinion, the peace-makers of our world (e.g., Martin Luther King, Jr., Nelson Mandela, Gandhi, Johan Galtung, Mairead McGuire, Glenn Paige, and so many more) are spiritual leaders. They were driven by beliefs and actions transcending the times their lives, in favor of broader social concerns and timeless spiritual connections.

The term "spirituality" should not be limited to "ecclesiastical" contexts. Media popularity has liberated the term making it possible to be "spiritual" without being associated with or being a member of particular religion. The term "secular spirituality," has emerged to describe non-materialistic individuals or ways-of-being that are not necessarily associated with membership or belief in a formal religion.

In my opinion, this is good! In a world dominated by Western commercial cultural traditions and values that emphasize materialism, consumerism, production, and commodification, a concern for the "spiritual" serves as a powerful counter-point for defining the meaning and value of life beyond the "collected junk" that adorns our lives yet leaves us feeling unfulfilled. We sense our discontent, but too often, we fail to recognize its source in "meaninglessness," and we simply continue to accumulate more and more goods. Materialism can become an addiction. We are driven to consume (i.e., buy, eat, collect) as a source of comfort and anxiety reduction.

Okay, what can we do? It is difficult to escape the daily pressures to consume. We have just completed a holiday in which extravagances in purchases and consumption dominated our lives. However, when people say: "I begin to be excited just anticipating "Black Friday" (i.e., the day after Thanksgiving reputed to be largest shopping day) and/or "Self Day" (i.e., the day after Christmas day when goods are exchanged and gift cards used)." Something needs to be corrected.

I do not choose a medieval monastic life for myself, nor do I advocate the same for others. I see the virtues and appeal in complete social detachment and silence, but I think meaning is best found in pursuing inner and outer paths. I am not free from materialistic impulses, nor am I free of the comforts materialism provides. Clearly, I am privileged to have access to the material comforts in our society. But this does not mean I cannot strive to understand and experience "spirituality" in my life.

It is a special privilege to reflect, contemplate, ponder, meditate, and explore the nature of spirituality, and the possibilities of leading a spiritual life. To that end, I am attaching some of my personal guidelines for leading a spiritual life. I do not claim they are absolutes. They are merely thoughts I have found useful in pursuing a state of spirituality. I consider these guidelines to be consistent with all religions, and they are offered with respect for organized all religions. I offer five specific actions.

GUIDELINES FOR LIVING A SPIRITUAL LIFE

1. Awareness

I resolve to be more aware and responsive to the spiritual dimensions of my being and my nature. I intend to accept and to embrace the self-evident truth that the very life force that is within me is the same life force that moves, propels, and governs the universe itself, and because of this, I must approach life with a new sense of awe, humbled by the mystery of this truth, yet elated and confident by its consequences. I am alive! I am part of life! And, because of this, I must act in ways that encourage and support this fact, and I must act in ways that are responsive to its requirements and demands.

2. Cultivation of the Spirit

Because I am both an individual and a collective part of the life force that moves, propels, and governs the universe, I have serious responsibilities including acting and behaving in ways that sustain life in all its forms. I have an individual responsibility to do this. To this end, **I resolve to perfect the spiritual dimension of my being because it is in this pursuit that I can discover and fulfill my unique destiny in the larger cosmic plan whose details remain unknown, but whose intent seems clear -- the promotion of an evolutionary harmony, balance, and synergy among all life forms.** To this end, I intend to do all I can to fulfill and actualize my potential as a human being conscious of the power of choice and conscious of the virtue of cultivating the enduring life values of peace, beauty, truth, justice, and civility.

3. Living in the Passions of Our Time

Because spiritual maturity and perfection must be pursued through behavior, **I resolve to actively participate in the world in which I live, and to be a force for life through the conscious support of those people, ideas, and institutions that serve life through humanistic action.** To this end, I intend to live within the passions of my time, and not to be a passive bystander. I intend to make a difference in solving those life problems and challenges I can, whether they be big or small, using whenever possible the very energies generated by these challenges to derive my strength and determination.

4. Promoting Life

Because humanistic action is a pathway to spiritual perfection, and because the pursuit of spiritual perfection is the pathway revealing my place and role in the larger cosmic destiny and order, **I resolve to commit myself to those beliefs and actions that will illuminate, affirm, and promote the value and power of life,** including: **(1)** A recognition of the interdependency of all things; **(2)** A recognition of the importance of the process or way we do things rather than simply the product or outcome; **(3)** A recognition of the importance of promoting inner and outer peace as a means of promoting and preserving life; **(4)** An appreciation of beauty in all its manifestations and forms and, **(5)** A fostering of the impulse to penetrate into the nature of things for the sheer delight of inquiry, without any need to conquer or to subdue that which is learned.

5. Constant Renewal

Because the spiritual dimension of life is at once the most self-evident dimension of our being, and simultaneously the most hidden and mysterious, **I resolve to constantly acknowledge my spiritual nature, to revel in it, to preserve it, and to renew it, so all of my thoughts and behaviors will reflect and appreciate the simple yet profound joy of this truth.**

Note: These guidelines were first published as part of other articles in Marsella, A.J. (1994). They also appeared in "Making Important New Year Resolutions." Honolulu Star Bulletin, December 30, p. 10; Marsella, A.J. (1999). *In search of meaning: Some thoughts on belief, doubt, and wellbeing.* The International Journal of Transpersonal Studies, 18, 41-52, and in March, 2011, in Transcend Media Services (www.transcend.org).

Author Autobiography Notes

January 1, 2016

Anthony J. Marsella received his B.A. degree with Honors in Psychology from Baldwin-Wallace College, Berea, Ohio, in 1962; an M.A. in physiological psychology from Kent State University in 1964; and a Ph.D. in Clinical Psychology from Pennsylvania State University, University Park, Pennsylvania, in 1968. He also completed studies in cultural anthropology and philosophy of science at the doctoral level. After completing an internship at Worcester State Hospital, Worcester, Massachusetts, he received an appointment as a Fulbright Research Scholar to Ateneo de Manila University, Quezon City, Philippines, where he taught and conducted research on social stress and psychopathology in urban Manila. He subsequently served as field research director for a large-scale psychiatric epidemiological survey in the jungles of Sarawak (Borneo) designed to determine rates of mental illness among Chinese, Malay, and Iban (an indigenous tribal group) populations. Following a post-doctoral year as a Culture and Mental Health Fellow at the East-West Center/SSRI in Honolulu, he was appointed to the faculty of the Department of Psychology at the University of Hawai'i, a position he held until he retired in 2003.

Dr. Marsella is currently *Emeritus* Professor of Psychology and Past Director of the World Health Organization Psychiatric Research Center in Honolulu, Past Director of the Clinical Studies Program, and Past Director of the Disaster Management and Humanitarian Assistance Program at the University of Hawai'i. He served as Vice President for Academic Affairs at the University of Hawai'i in 1985-1989. Dr. Marsella has served as a consultant to numerous national and international agencies and organizations. He has been a visiting professor in Australia (Melbourne University and Monash University), Korea (Korea University, Seoul, Korea), India (King George Medical College, Lucknow, India), China (Shanghai Psychiatric Institute, Shanghai, China), and the Philippines (Ateneo de Manila University, Quezon City, Philippines). In addition, he has been a visiting professor at the Johns Hopkins University (Baltimore, Maryland), Clemson University (Clemson, South Carolina), and a visiting lecturer at numerous national and international universities and research centers. He is Past President of the Psychologists for Social Responsibility **(www.PsySR.org).**

Dr. Marsella has published nineteen books and more than 325 journal articles, technical reports, book reviews, and popular press/media service articles. He has been awarded numerous research and training grants and contracts in the areas of cross-cultural psychopathology and psychotherapy, PTSD, social stress and coping, schizophrenia, disasters, and the global challenges of our times. Much of his current writing is on peace and social justice. He serves currently on seven journal editorial boards and scientific and professional advisory committees. He was an associate editor for the *Corsini Encyclopedia of Psychology* (John Wiley & Sons) and was one of twelve senior editors for the *Encyclopedia of Psychology* (Oxford University Press/American Psychological Association). He currently serves as senior editor for the cultural and international psychology book series for Springer SBM Publications (New York), a thirty-seven volume series helping to define this important area of inquiry.

Dr. Marsella is widely known nationally and internationally as a pioneer figure in the study of culture, psychology, and psychopathology, who challenged the ethnocentric and racial biases of many assumptions, theories, methods, and practices in psychology and psychiatry. One of his frequently cited papers on "global-community psychology," published in the *American Psychologist*, December 1998, calls for the development of a new psychology relevant and responsive to the challenges of our global era, including the internationalization of the psychology curriculum. In more recent years, Dr. Marsella has written extensively on the challenges of war and peace in our global era, calling for all people to recognize they are first a manifestation of life itself, *Lifeism.* This recognition carries responsibilities, obligations, and duties to and for others and our Earth.

Dr. Marsella directed 96 doctoral dissertations and masters theses and served as a committee member on scores of others during the course of his 35-year career at the University of Hawai'i. He received the *College of Social Sciences Award for Teaching Excellence* and was selected by the American Psychological Association as a *Master Lecturer* in 1994 for his contributions in cross-cultural psychology and psychopathology. Also in 1994, he was selected as the *Best Teacher* in the "Best of Manoa Student Poll" at the University of Hawai'i. The Hawaii Psychological Association (HPA) selected Dr. Marsella for its *Significant Professional Contribution Award* for his scholarly and professional achievements in 1996, and, in 2004, the Hawaii Psychological Association presented him with its *Lifetime Achievement Award.* He received the *Alumni Merit Award* from his *alma mater,* Baldwin-Wallace College, and was subsequently selected as the first recipient of the *Kathryn Grover Harrington Scholar Award* from Baldwin-Wallace College. He received the *Medal of Highest Honor* from Soka University in Tokyo, Japan, for his contributions to the academy and to the promotion of international peace and understanding.

In 1996, the American Psychological Association selected Dr. Marsella for the *Distinguished Contributions to the International Advancement of Psychology Award.* He was listed in Who's Who in America in 1996. In November 1999, he was awarded an honorary doctorate degree — *Doctoris Honoris Causa* — by the University of Copenhagen, Copenhagen, Denmark, at a ceremony presided over by Queen Margrette II. In 2003, Psychologists for Social Responsibility (PsySR) created an annual *Anthony J. Marsella Prize for Peace and Social Justice,* in honor of his work.

Dr. Marsella was awarded the *International Psychologist of the Year Award* by Division 52 of the American Psychological Association in 2004. Additionally in 2004, the Asian American Psychological Association awarded him the Presidential Award for contributions to Asian Americans. In 2007, he received the *Outstanding Retired Faculty Award* from the College of Social Sciences at the University of Hawai'i. In August 2009, he was presented with the *International Academy of Intercultural Research Lifetime Achievement Award*, and, in 2010, he was awarded the *International Mentoring Award* from APA Division 52. He received the *Columbia University Teachers' College Counselors Roundtable Award for Distinguished Contributions to Peace and Social Justice* in February 2012. In August 2012, the International Section of the APA Division of Counseling presented him with its *Lifetime Achievement Award* for contributions to internationalizing counseling psychology. In June 2013, he was selected as one of twelve pioneers in the field of multicultural counseling and psychology and invited to submit an autobiographical article in the forthcoming publication of *The Handbook of Multicultural Counseling;* in addition, he has been asked to submit a profile of his life in a forthcoming volume on courage and risk among psychologists.

Dr. Marsella now lives in Atlanta, Georgia, USA, where he continues to lecture and write. He currently enjoys reading, writing, cooking, and learning about life — its many complexities, beauties, and sorrows — from people he meets along the way. In his older age, he has taken up writing poetry, lyrics, and short stories (e.g., *Poems across Time and Place: A Journey of Heart and Mind (see Amazon.com)*. This volume is his nineteenth book publication – the volume shares intimate narratives of his life.

Anthony J. Marsella, Ph.D., *D.H.C.*
Professor *Emeritus*
University of Hawai'i
Honolulu, Hawai'i
marsella@hawaii.edu